@ jaxon~ THONHOFF

- LA BAHIA (GOLIAD)
- SAN ROSARIO
- CAMINO a LAREDO
- REFUGIO (1793)
- PASTURE LANDS OF ROSARIO UNTIL 1899
- SAN ROSARIO
- Aransas
- PISCINA
- SAN ANTONIO
- Nueces
- SAN PATRICIO
- LA BAHIA de CORPUS CHRISTI

LEGEND:

■ SAN ANTONIO de BEXAR • FOUNDED IN 1718

① MISSION SAN ANTONIO de VALERO (THE ALAMO) • 1718

② MISSION PURISIMA CONCEPTION • 1731

③ MISSION SAN JOSE de AGUAYO • 1720

④ MISSION SAN JUAN CAPISTRANO • 1731

⑤ MISSION SAN FRANCISCO de la ESPADA • 1731

⑥ LAS ISLITAS • SETTLEMENT OF CANARY ISLANDERS, LOCATED NEAR "SHEEP CROSSING", ON PRESENT ROAD TO ELMENDORF.

⑦• PASO de MALDONADO • POSSIBLY NAMED FOR MALDONADO FAMILY. NEAR PRESENT GRAYTOWN.

⑧• PRESENT DAY FLORESVILLE, NAMED FOR FAMILY OF FRANCISCO FLORES de ABREGO y VALDES, WHO OWNED LOS CHAYOPINES.

■• RUINS OF LAS CABRAS RANCH CHAPEL. THE "GOAT RANCH" WAS OWNED BY MISSION ESPADA, AND LATER BY MANUEL BARRERA.

8• CONQUISTA CROSSING • NEAR PRESENT FALLS CITY.

PATAGUILLA • NAMED FOR INDIANS OF MISSION SAN JUAN, WHO ONCE HAD THIS RANCH.

9• RUINS OF PUERTE del SANTA CRUZ de CIBOLO, AS EARLY AS 1788 DON ANDRES HERNANDEZ BUILT HEADQUARTERS FOR HIS RANCH SAN BARTOLO NEARBY.

OJTOS de SANTA CRUZ • "HOLY CROSS SPRINGS". NOW SUTHERLAND SPRINGS.

SAN LUCAS • OWNED BY DOMINGO CASTELO HEIRS.

PASO de los MUJERES • "WOMEN'S CROSSING". OWNED BY CALVILLO HEIRS.

SAN FRANCISCO • OWNED BY LUIS MENCHACA HEIRS.

LAS MULAS • VICENTE ALVAREZ TRAVIESO HEIRS.

LAGUNA de las ANIMAS • OWNED BY THE DELGADOS, THEN ZAMBRANOS. "LAGOON OF THE SPIRITS" BECAME PROPERTY OF GASPAR FLORES IN 1835.

LA MORA, "MULBERRY RANCH", OWNED BY MISSION SAN ANTONIO de VALERO, GRANTED TO ERASMO SEGUIN IN 1834. HIS RANCH HOUSE "CASA BLANCA" HOWEVER, WAS UP BY PRESENT FLORESVILLE, MARRIED A ...

SAN ANTONIO del CIBOLO AND "BURNT WOOD" RANCHES • THE GRANADO– de ARMAS HEIRS.

EL PASTLE • "MOSS RANCH", OWNED BY SEBASTIAN MONJARAS IN 1770? THEN BY BALMACEDAS.

RANCHO de las HERMANAS • "THE SISTERS RANCH", OWNED BY COUP ... URAN HEIRS.

EL ATASCOSA • RANCH OF MISSION SAN JOSE; TITLE RECEIVED ... SE ANTONIO

SAN RAFAEL • HEIRS OF SIMON AND JUAN de AROCHA ... NAVARRO.

LOS CORRALITOS • OWNED BY DON BERNABE CARIAJ ...

SEÑOR SAN JOSE • OWNED BY CARLOS MARTINEZ, K ... ESPIRITU SANTO.

RANCHO de CAPITAN PISCINA • RANCH OF LA BAHIA G ...

NOGALES • "WALNUTS"; A SETTLEMENT THAT BECAME V ... E "GOLIAD ROAD".

MISSION ESPIRITU SANTO AND PRESIDIO LA BAHIA MOVED ... TER. SEGUIN.

MISSION ROSARIO FOUNDED IN 1754. IT AND ESPIRITU SANTO ... IN 1749.

... S AND PASTURE LANDS.

(THIS MAP PREPARED WITH THE RESEARCH ... ROBERT H. THONHOFF)

This Texas Longhorn descendant is pastured on land once a part of the Rancho del Señor San José in present Karnes County, Texas. It weighs about 2400 lbs., and its horns are 84 in. tip to tip, close to, if not, a world record.

The
Texas
Connection

With The
American Revolution

By

Robert H. Thonhoff

EAKIN PRESS
AUSTIN, TEXAS

FIRST EDITION

Third Printing

Copyright © 1981
By Robert H. Thonhoff

Published in the United States of America
By Eakin Publications, Inc., P.O. Box 23066, Austin, Texas 78735

ISBN 0-89015-277-2

This book is dedicated to

"Boss" Mills

and his Barbershop Gang,

past and present,

of Karnes City, Texas.

75112

ACKNOWLEDGMENTS

A human being can accomplish very little by himself, but great accomplishments can be achieved when people help one another—so it is with this work. The author is deeply indebted to many people for their help in making this book possible.

Special thanks go to Jack Jackson, artist-historian of Austin, Texas, who collaborated with the author to produce the map of the Ranchos of the San Antonio River Valley—1780. *Muchas gracias* go to Robert S. Weddle of Austin, Texas, for all his help, encouragement, and suggestions for this book, which is a sequel to our book, *Drama & Conflict: The Texas Saga of 1776,* published in 1976. *Und danke schön, auch,* goes to Jess R. Richter, publisher of *The Karnes Citation* newspaper of Karnes City, Texas, for "helping a friend in need."

Much appreciation is due Mrs. Elizabeth Swize, County Clerk of Karnes County, Texas, and her staff, especially Mrs. Alva L. Jonas, for all her assistance. Special acknowledgement is extended to Dr. Chester Kielman, Bill Richter, Ralph Elder, Frances Rogers, and other staff members of the University of Texas at Austin Archives, where much of the research for this book was done. Deeply appreciated, also, is the wholehearted assistance of Jack Maguire and his friendly staff at the Institute of Texan Cultures in San Antonio, Texas.

Many thanks and much appreciation is extended to J.R. "Boss" Mills and that grand group of men who have frequented his barbershop in Karnes City, Texas. And, last but not least, much love is reciprocated to my dear wife, Victoria Balser Thonhoff, who has been so patient and understanding with me these past thirty years.

CONTENTS

Introduction vii

I. The Texas Setting 1

II. The Spanish Participation 19

III. The Texas Contribution 45

IV. Some Ramifications 73

Appendix 79

ILLUSTRATIONS

Texas Longhorn . . . . Frontispiece

New Spain at the Time of the
American Revolution, map 2

Texas in 1779, map 11

Bernardo de Gálvez 21

Vista de Panzacola y Su Baía 41

General Gálvez Before St. George,
May 8, 1781 43

Spain and the American Revolution 44

Cavalry Company of the Royal
Presidio of La Bahía del
Espíritu Santo, May 5, 1782 94

Ranchos of the San Antonio River
Valley—1780 . . . . (end papers)

INTRODUCTION

All too often, when Americans think of the American Revolution, they think only in terms of the events that occurred in the thirteen English colonies. Important as they were, they do not tell the whole story. An oft-neglected part of it concerns the role of Spain in the American Revolution. A generally unknown part of it is the Texas connection. Overlooked by most historians much too long, the contribution of Spain, Texas included, was vital in the winning of American independence two hundred years ago.

History must ever stand to be proved, improved, reproved, or disproved. This is as it should be. The story of man, like the ever-moving ocean sweeping sand on the beach, is an ever-changing phenomenon. Much of man's history has disappeared in the shifting sands of time, but historical researchers, like beachcombers, can still painstakingly look through dusty archival records and find new bits of information that have never been incorporated into history books.

Eminent authorities have generally neglected to mention anything positive in American Revolution history about Spain. For example, the much-quoted American Revolution historian Samuel F. Bemis made the following statement:

> . . . But we can point to little in the naval or military history of the war which shows [Spain's] operations helpful to the struggle which the United States and France were waging against England. The small flow of Spanish subsidies to America had little actual result; and, until further research into the effect of Spanish naval operations on the general history of the war has shown the contrary, it is reasonable to assume that the Spanish participation was not a decisive military factor in the achievement of American independence.[1]

1. Samuel Flagg Bemis, *The Diplomacy of the American Revolution* (Bloomington, Indiana, 1965), 111. First published in 1935, this much-quoted volume had its sixth printing in 1965.

A more recently published book by Jack M. Sosin in the well-known Histories of the American Frontier Series also negates Spain's contribution to the success of the American Revolution with this statement:

> . . . Clearly the efforts of the Spanish were limited to achieving their own aims on the Mississippi, and except for diverting some British and Indian manpower, they did not materially aid the American cause when the British between 1779 and 1781 directed their main effort against Georgia and the Carolinas.[2]

Other minimizing statements such as the following are offered by Latin American history authorities for general consumption:

> . . . Charles [III] aligned Spain with France in a war on England in 1779, thereby giving moral—though not military—aid to the North Americans in their unequal struggle with England.[3]

> . . . For the Spanish Empire, its support of the Anglo-American Revolution in 1779, surreptitious and indirect as it may have been, was also a confusing and unfortunate precedent.[4]

In what is considered by many to be the best and most comprehensive treatment of the American Revolution, John R. Alden's *A History of the American Revolution* devotes little

2. Jack M. Sosin, *The Revolutionary Frontier, 1763-1783* (New York, 1967), 126.

3. Hubert Herring, *A History of Latin America* (New York, 1965), 247. This has been a standard college textbook studied by countless thousands of university students since it was first published in 1955.

4. Hugh M. Hamill, *The Hidalgo Revolt: Prelude to Mexican Independence* (Gainesville, Florida, 1966), 9.

more than one page out of more than five hundred pages in the book to the military exploits of Bernardo de Gálvez, who led the Spanish military and naval campaign against the British in North America.[5] Alden's previously published New American Nation Series book entitled *The American Revolution, 1775-1783* contains exactly one sentence about Gálvez,[6] certainly an unheralded hero of the American Revolution whose name should rightfully rank with those of Lafayette, de Grasse, Rochambeau, von Steuben, de Kalb, Pulaski, and Kosciusko.

The foregoing are just a few prime examples of history books that make brief, passive mention of Spain's role in the American Revolution. Most books on American and Latin American history say nothing. This includes officially adopted state textbooks on American and Texas history for Texas school children. To this date, not one has been published that mentions Gálvez, much less the Texas participation in the American Revolution.

One wonders why there is, at worst, such a dearth of information or, at best, such a minimization of information about Spain's role in the American Revolution. Perhaps one of the reasons is that most writers of the American Revolution have been from the Northeast, and as such they have presented only the Northeast perspective from the records available to them. By not having examined the voluminous Spanish records for the period, they have unwittingly and unknowingly omitted an integral part to the American Revolution story. Some authors, whose works have long been considered the last and final words on the subject, have made erroneous statements that not only have been accepted without question but, worst of all, have been perpetuated as truth.

This is not meant to judge or condemn any historian for what is written or not written; rather, it is to point out the fact that we yet have much to write about in history. In this case,

5. John R. Alden, *A History of the American Revolution* (New York, 1969), 430-431.

6. John R. Alden, *The American Revolution, 1775-1783* (New York, 1954), 239.

much awaits the researcher in the voluminous Spanish archival records that are scattered all over the world. Once fully examined, they will throw new light on the interesting and exciting American Revolution period, which had momentous, world-wide effects.

One of the first to perceive the greatness and the significance of Bernardo de Gálvez was John Walton Caughey, a student of Herbert E. Bolton. Caughey, using original Spanish documents, wrote a book entitled *Bernardo de Gálvez in Louisiana, 1776-1783*, which was published by the University of California in 1934. Caughey's work has gone unnoticed until recently, and it appears that "its time has arrived." It is refreshing, for example, to see regional scholars such as Jack D.L. Holmes revitalize Caughey's work in Holmes's book *Honor and Fidelity* (Birmingham, 1965). Another welcome revision to American Revolution history, giving Spanish and Gálvez due credit, is the book by J. Leitch Wright, Jr., entitled *Anglo-Spanish Rivalry in North America* (University of Georgia Press, Athens, 1971). And, happily, Caughey's *Bernardo de Gálvez in Louisiana, 1776-1783* was reprinted in 1972 by the Pelican Publishing Company of Gretna, Louisiana. Hopefully, there will be more works of these kinds available for the needed revision of our general history books.

The story that follows adds a new dimension to the history of Texas and the history of the American Revolution. As much as they did for American and Texas history, men such as Herbert E. Bolton, Eugene C. Barker, Carlos E. Castañeda, Walter Prescott Webb, and H. Bailey Carroll did not have time to pursue all historical topics to finality. Much was left for others. Herewith is a story, based on recent research of original Spanish documents in the Bexar Archives at the University of Texas at Austin, that will place the history of Texas and the history of the American Revolution in an exciting, new perspective.

The Texas Connection

With the American Revolution

I

THE TEXAS SETTING

At the time of the American Revolution, Spain owned or claimed all the land of the North American continent west of the Mississippi River plus the New Orleans portion of Louisiana. This vast territory was called *Nueva España* (New Spain), which in turn was divided into *provincias* (provinces).

Five northernmost provinces extended into the area known today as the State of Texas. *La Provincia de Nuevo México* (New Mexico), whose capital was Santa Fé, included the area around El Paso. The Big Bend area was a part of *La Provincia de Nueva Vizcaya* (New Biscay), whose capital was Chihuahua. The region along the Río Grande between the Big Bend and Laredo belonged to *La Provincia de Nueva Estremadura* (New Estremadura, most often called Coahuila), whose capital was Monclova. A long strip of land from the Río Pánuco on the south to the Nueces River on the north and from the Gulf Coast as far inland as Laredo belonged to *La Provincia de Nuevo Santander* (New Santander), whose capital was at San Carlos.[1] Excepting Nuevo Santander, these first four provinces were open-ended and had no fixed boundary on the north.

The fifth province, formally called *La Provincia de Texas* ó *Las Nuevas Filipinas* (the Province of Texas or the New Philippines), extended from the Nueces River on the south and west to the Red River on the north and east, and from the Gulf Coast on the south to the "Arctic snows" on the north—quite a chunk of territory that would theoretically include much of the United States and Canada. Practically speaking, however, the plains Indians imposed limits that were unequivocal. From 1721

1. Cf. Robert S. Weddle and Robert H. Thonhoff, *Drama & Conflict: The Texas Saga of 1776* (Austin, Texas, 1976), 14.

THIRTEEN COLONIES

Ohio

Mississippi

West Florida

East Florida

New Orleans

NEW SPAIN
At The Time Of The
American Revolution

NEW SPAIN

to 1773, the capital of the Province of Texas was at Los Adaes, near present Robeline, Louisiana. From 1773 till 1821, the end of the Spanish colonial period, the capital was at San Antonio de Béxar.

During the period of the American Revolution, Spain was a ranking world power. Her king was King Carlos III, an enlightened divine-right monarch, who governed with the assistance of an able ministry. The son of Philip V and the half-brother of Ferdinand VI, Carlos III was the third Bourbon to occupy the Spanish throne. By the end of the Hapsburg dynasty, 1516-1700, Spain had declined, but the reign of Carlos III, sometimes called "the best of the Bourbons," brought it back to heights of glory and achievement not seen since the sixteenth century.

The stature of Carlos III is enhanced further when one considers some of his European monarchical contemporaries: King George III, of the House of Hanover, in England; King Louis XVI, of the House of Bourbon, in France; Maria Theresa, of the House of Hapsburg, Empress of the Holy Roman Empire; Frederick the Great, of the House of Hohenzollern, of Prussia; Catherine the Great, of the House of Romanov, of Russia; and King Gustav III of Sweden.[2] And it is interesting to note that the present King of Spain, Juan Carlos Victor María de Borbón y Borbón, who ascended to the throne of Spain at the end of the thirty-six year rule of Francisco Franco in 1975, is a direct descendant of Carlos III.

Assisting the king in colonial rule was a Council of the Indies, formally termed the *Real y Supremo Consejo de las Indias,* which exercised extensive executive, legislative, and judicial powers. A codified body of law called the *Recopilación de Leyes de las Reinos de las Indias,* commonly called the Laws of the Indies, governed the lives of all Spanish colonial subjects in minute detail.[3]

2. For a synopsis of European monarchical families, cf. the genealogical tables in Carleton J.H. Hayes, *A Political and Cultural History of Modern Europe* (2 vols., New York, 1947).

3. Cf. C.H. Haring, *The Spanish Empire in America* (New York, 1947) for a very fine description of Spanish colonial government.

The Indies were divided into two viceroyalties, New Spain and Perú. Extending northward from Guatemala, New Spain included the big half of the North American continent west of the Mississippi River, New Orleans, and the Spanish-owned islands of the Greater Antilles. The chief agent of the King of Spain in the New World was the viceroy. During the three-century-long colonial period, sixty-two viceroys, representing many of Spain's noblest and most distinguished families, ruled New Spain. One of the most efficient was Viceroy Antonio María Bucareli y Ursúa, usually called Viceroy Bucareli, who served from 1771 to 1779. Succeeding Viceroy Bucareli during the American Revolution years were Martín de Mayorga (1779-1783) and Matías de Gálvez (1783-1784), father of Bernardo de Gálvez, of whom more is said later.

Power under Spanish law emanated from the king and filtered downward intricately through the Council of the Indies to the viceroys, captains-general, audiencias, and finally to the governors of the provinces. Each *gobernador*, or governor, owed his office to royal appointment. In his dual role as governor of the province and captain of the presidio in the capital, he exercised both civil and military authority. The Province of Texas during the years of the American Revolution was governed by Juan María Vicencio, Barón de Ripperdá (1770-1778) and Domingo Cabello (1778-1786).

Another officer that became very instrumental in the affairs of Texas during these years was the commandant of the line of *presidios* (forts) along the northern frontier of New Spain. A royal order called *Reglamento e instrucción para los presidios que han forman en la línea de frontera de la Nueva España* was issued by Carlos III on September 10, 1772. These "New Regulations" created the *provincias internas*, or Interior Provinces, of New Spain (California, Sonora, Sinaloa, New Mexico, Nueva Vizcaya, Coahuila, Nuevo Leon, Nuevo Santander, and Texas) and placed them under the authority of a military governor, who exercised civil, judicial, and military power. To provide a defensive cordon, fifteen presidios were established as equidistantly as possible in a zigzag line that extended from the

4

Gulf of California on the west to the Gulf of Mexico on the east. The presidios at San Antonio de Béxar and La Bahía formed a part of this new arrangement. In command of all these forts during the period of this study were *Comandante-Inspector* Hugo Oconór (1772-1777) and *Comandante-General* Teodoro de Croix (1777-1783).[4]

Monarchical government finally trickled down to the towns-people of New Spain in a system considerably more sophisticated than most people realize. Most often we give the English sole credit for our present form of government, but a number of antecedents were established, also, by Spanish government. The Villa de San Fernando de Béxar, for example, became the civil settlement adjoining the Presidio San Antonio de Béxar in 1731. Since that time it has had its own form of local government. A city council called the *cabildo* was composed of six councilmen called *regidores* and two mayors called *alcaldes*. Other city officials included the chief constable or *alguacil mayor*, the *síndico or city attorney, the fiscal* or city treasurer, the *escribano* or city secretary, the *mayordomo* or custodian of city property, and the *curador de memores* or city archivist.[5] Thus continues the modern City of San Antonio today.

In the Province of Texas were the presidios at San Antonio de Béxar, at La Bahía (now Goliad), and the outpost between them called El Fuerte del Cíbolo (Fort Cibolo, established near present Czestochowa in Karnes County). There were but three civil settlements during the American Revolution years: the Villa de San Fernando de Béxar (now San Antonio); the settlement that grew around Presidio La Bahía (now Goliad); and the temporary displaced person settlement of the Villa de Bucareli (1774-1779, near present Antioch in Madison County), which

---

4. Odie B. Faulk, *The Last Years of Spanish Texas* (The Hague, 1964), 18-19.

5. For a detailed account of the operation of government in Texas, cf. Mattie Austin Hatcher, "The Municipal Government of San Fernando de Bexar, 1730-1800," *The Quarterly of the Texas State Historical Association,* VIII (April, 1905).

was moved in 1779 to become the Villa de Nacogdoches.[6]

Established since 1718, the Presidio de San Antonio de Béxar occupied present Military Plaza in San Antonio. Monthly military rosters, of which only a few are extant, for the years 1779 to 1782 show a troop strength that varied between 81 and 106 officers and enlisted men. An open post not built along classical stockade lines, Presidio San Antonio de Béxar was commanded by the governor of Texas, who also held the title of captain of the presidio. During these years, the governor resided in a group of buildings called the *Casas Reales,* or Royal Buildings, on the east side of present Main Plaza, opposite San Fernando Cathedral. The site is a parking lot today. The building now called the Spanish Governor's Palace was then the residence of the senior ranking officer of the presidio, Lieutenant Josef Félix Menchaca, of whom more will be said later. Besides the captain, there were usually a first lieutenant, a second lieutenant, a first ensign, a second ensign, two or three sergeants, six to eight corporals, and seventy to ninety soldiers. In any given month, about one-fourth of these men were present for duty at the presidio; another quarter were detached to the horse herd; about one-fourth were reconnoitering for Indians; about twenty men were stationed at El Fuerte del Cíbolo to guard the ranches; and four to seven men escorted the mail and military payroll. By 1780, the soldiers were designated as being *Tropa de Cuera* ("Leather Troops," distinguished by their leather jackets) or *Tropa de Ligera* ("Light Troops," equipped so that they could dismount easily and engage the enemy in hand to hand combat).[7]

Founded in 1731 for the Canary Island immigrants, the Villa de San Fernando de Béxar grew around the presidio. Canary Island families, soldiers of the presidio and their

6. Cf. Herbert E. Bolton, *Texas in the Middle Eighteenth Century* (New York, 1962), and Weddle and Thonhoff, *Drama & Conflict: The Texas Saga of 1776* for descriptions of these settlements in the 1770's.

7. Cf. the various monthly rosters for the Presidio San Antonio de Béxar in the Bexar Archives for the years 1779 to 1782 in the Archives of the University of Texas at Austin.

families, and other settlers resided in homes built on lots in blocks lined by streets determined by survey. The first official census for the Province of Texas in 1783 (seven years before the first census of the United States!) listed a total of 1248 persons living in the Presidio San Antonio de Béxar and its civil settlement of San Fernando de Béxar. Of these, 331 were men, 311 women, 321 boys, 264 girls, 8 men slaves, and 13 women slaves.[8]

Five missions were situated near the presidio and villa. Mission San Antonio de Valero (now called The Alamo) had 149 persons living there in 1783. Further down the San Antonio River, in order, were Mission Nuestra Señora de la Purísima Concepción with 87, Mission San José y San Miguel de Aguayo with 123, Mission San Juan Capistrano with 99, and Mission San Francisco de la Espada with 96 inhabitants.[9]

Presidio Nuestra Señora de Loreto de la Bahía, usually called Presidio La Bahía, had been moved to its third and final site in 1749 on the west bank of the San Antonio River near present Goliad. Nearby were established the two missions of Nuestra Señora del Espíritu Santo de Zúñiga, usually called Mission Espíritu Santo, and Nuestra Señora del Rosario, usually called Mission Rosario.

In 1779 Presidio La Bahía showed a troop strength of 53 men, broken down as follows: one captain, one lieutenant, one ensign, one sergeant, two corporals, and forty-seven privates. By May 1, 1782, the monthly rosters show that the troop strength had increased to 69 men, broken down as follows: one captain, two lieutenants, two ensigns, two sergeants, eight corporals, one drummer, and fifty-two privates. The troops *de cuera* listed 29 men; the troops *de ligera* had 33 men.[10]

The 1783 census lists 454 persons residing at Presidio La Bahía: 193 men, 147 women, 68 boys, 45 girls, and 1 male slave. Mission Espíritu Santo had 214 persons living there in

8. Report showing the Number of Subjects and Inhabitants the King Has in This Province, Distinguished by Class, Marital Status, and Race, All Persons of Both Sexes, Including Children, December 31, 1783, Bexar Archives.

9. *Ibid.*

10. Cf. the infrequent monthly rosters for the Presidio La Bahía in the Bexar Archives for the years 1779 to 1782.

1783. Mission Rosario, abandoned a year or two earlier, showed none. In the environs of Presidio La Bahía, therefore, could be counted six to seven hundred persons, a considerable settlement for the time.[11]

The small settlement of Villa de Nuestra Señora del Pilar de Bucareli, usually called the Villa de Bucareli, existed only from 1774 to 1779. Its twice-transplanted Adaesano settlers were evicted a third time by fire, flood, and Indians in the spring of 1779. Then the East Texas settlers "folded their tents like Arabs and silently stole away" back to their old homeland, where they established the Villa de Nuestra Señora del Pilár de los Nacogdoches. The Villa de Nacogdoches had 349 people living there according to the census of 1783. Of these, 129 were men, 104 women, 52 boys, 50 girls, 8 men slaves, and 6 women slaves.[12] The leader of the settlement was Don Antonio Gil Ybarbo, who was *justicia mayor* (chief justice) of the villa, captain of the militia, and lieutenant governor of the Province of Texas.

In all, there were 2819 people enumerated as Spanish subjects in the Province of Texas in the census of 1783. An interesting feature of the census was that each person was identified by class or caste, reflecting the significance to such considerations. The caste designation came immediately after the name: Spaniard, Frenchman, mestizo, mulatto, lobo (Indian-mulatto cross), coyote (Indian-mestizo cross), Indian, or slave. Pride of lineage, inherent in the Spaniard as in other Europeans, was carried abroad even to the frontier Province of Texas.[13]

At the time of the American Revolution, that portion of Texas lying below the Nueces River and east of Laredo comprised the northern portion of the Province of Nuevo Santander, established in 1749 by the great colonizer José de Escandón. Six of the twenty-three towns that he founded lay along the Río

11. Census Report, December 31, 1783, Bexar Archives.
12. *Ibid.*
13. One of the best descriptions of the caste system in Texas and New Spain is found in Pedro Alonso O'Crouley, *A Description of the Kingdom of New Spain, 1774,* translated and edited by Sean Galvin (San Francisco, 1972).

Grande: on the right bank were Camargo and Reynosa (1749), Revilla (1750), and Mier (1752); on the left bank were Dolores (1750) and Laredo (1755). In addition to town lots, settlers of these Río Grande villages were granted farm and ranch lands called *porciones,* that fronted on either side of the river. Starting in the 1770's, huge royal land grants were made to prominent citizens of the villas. By that time the entire region was fairly well populated by people whose economy was based on raising livestock, especially sheep.[14]

Adjoining the provinces of Nuevo Santander and Texas on the west was the Province of Nuevo Estremadura, commonly called Coahuila. Up the Río Grande about eighty miles, on the right bank, was its northernmost settlement, San Juan Bautista, the progenitor of many Texas settlements. Founded in 1700, this outpost and gateway to Texas in 1779 had a presidio, two missions, and a settlement that extended along both sides of the river. A number of ranches surrounded this village of about eight hundred people.[15]

The jurisdiction of Nueva Vizcaya extended across the Río Grande to embrace the region of La Junta de los Ríos in the Big Bend. The settlement that grew around Presidio del Norte and the missions at La Junta, now the site of Ojinaga, Chihuahua, was never large. Mission Indians and Spanish settlers apparently engaged in some farming and ranching on both sides of the river.[16]

Settled since 1680, the El Paso area had a large population of Spaniards, mestizos, and Indians. Presidio del Paso del Norte and Presidio San Eleazario, both established by the New Regulations of 1772, provided protection for the settlers. Numerous land grants were made to citizens living around the

14. The multi-volume *Acts of the General Visit* in the Spanish Archives of the General Land Office in Austin, Texas, have the original surveys of Reynosa, Camargo, Mier, Revilla, and Laredo, as well as references to Dolores.

15. Cf. Robert S. Weddle, *San Juan Bautista: Gateway to Spanish Texas* (Austin, Texas, 1968).

16. Howard G. Applegate and C. Wayne Hanselka, *La Junta de los Ríos Del Norte y Conchos,* Southwestern Studies Monograph Number 41 (El Paso, Texas, 1974), 15-23.

missions at San Lorenzo, Senecú, Ysleta, and Socorro. Belonging to the Province of New Mexico, this entire region was bustling with activity: fairs were held, bargains were struck, horses were traded, and horsehides, cured sheepskins, and buffalo robes were bought and sold.[17]

Today, people all over the world, thanks to Hollywood and TV, know about the great cattle drives out of Texas in the years following the Civil War. But very few people are aware of the fact that ranching and trail driving got their start in Texas long before that time. Indeed, Spanish ranching activity had reached astonishing proportions in the 1770's and 1780's, and it extended across Texas, leap-frog fashion, from El Paso on the west to Nacogdoches on the east.

Volume after volume of old Spanish records in the Bexar Archives are filled with documents that relate to ranching activities in Spanish Texas two hundred years ago. Most of them pertain to the Béxar-La Bahía area of South Texas, which became the nucleus of the famed "Cattle Kingdom" that developed after the Civil War. Other documents, however, show that ranching was not confined to the Béxar-La Bahía region; rather, it was also carried on extensively in other areas across present Texas: on both sides of the Sabine River near Nacogdoches; along both sides of the Trinity River in the vicinity of Bucareli; on both sides of the lower Río Grande, extending northward to the Nueces River; and along the upper reaches of the Río Grande in the La Junta and El Paso areas. So vitally important was the *rancho* in Spanish Texas that it ranks with the *presidio, mission,* and *villa* as basic institutions used by Spain to settle Texas during her period of ownership.[18]

Probably the best description of the famed "Cattle Kingdom" was that made by the late Walter Prescott Webb in his book entitled *The Great Plains*. Webb delineated the "Cat-

17. O'Crouley, *A Description of the Kingdom of New Spain*, 51-52.

18. For a detailed picture of ranching activity in Texas during the eighteenth century, cf. Chapter 8, "The Birth of a Tradition," in Weddle and Thonhoff, *Drama & Conflict: The Texas Saga of 1776*, 143-171.

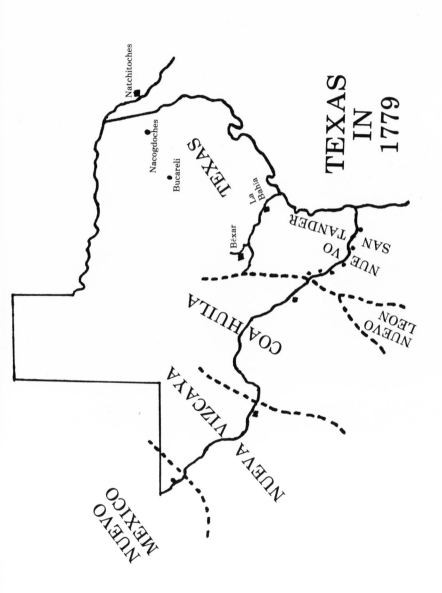

TEXAS
IN
1779

Natchitoches

Nacogdoches

Bucareli

TEXAS

La
Bahía

Béxar

NUEVO
SANTANDER

SAN

NUEVO
LEÓN

COAHUILA

NUEVA VIZCAYA

NUEVO
MÉXICO

11

tle Kingdom" as being "a diamond-shaped region" in South Texas bound by lines between San Antonio, Old Indianola, Brownsville, and Laredo. This region offered almost perfect conditions for the raising of livestock: the country was open; grass was plentiful; water was sufficient; and the climate was mild. It was a natural place where men on horseback could manage cattle.[19]

Forming the nucleus of this extensive region of South Texas was the area between present San Antonio and Goliad. The rich ranching region that stretched along the San Antonio, Cíbolo, and Guadalupe river valleys was filled with countless thousands of head of cattle, horses, mules, donkeys, sheep, and goats. In this region, as the end paper map illustrates, were numerous private ranches belonging to individuals who had received them by royal land grant. Most of the land not privately owned belonged to the five missions at San Antonio or to the two missions at La Bahía. Most significant for the story told here is the fact that Spanish ranching was nearing its zenith in this birthplace of ranching at the time of the American Revolution.

Situated along the banks of the San Antonio River, the five missions of San Antonio had been given in 1731 huge, vaguely defined grants of land that extended outward from the river, which was generally used as the axis and base line for the partitions. The land given to San Antonio de Valero extended generally from the immediate area around the mission to the east and northeast. However, because of its first location on the west side of the river near San Pedro Creek, it also had lands to the west and northwest of the river. The grant made to Concepción, the next mission down the river, also on the east bank, extended eastward to the Río Cíbolo, encompassing in all fifteen square leagues of land. (One square league amounted to 4,428 acres.) A little further down the river, but on the west bank, was San José, whose lands extended west and southwest into present Medina and Atascosa counties. Next downriver, on the east bank, was San Juan Capistrano, whose lands adjoined those belonging to Concepción on the north and included most of the

19. Walter Prescott Webb, *The Great Plains* (Boston, 1931), 208-210.

land between the La Bahía Road and the Arroyo del Cíbolo. A little further down the river, on the west bank, was San Francisco de la Espada, whose pastures generally took in the land from the west bank of the river to the Laredo Road, which separated them from those of San José.[20]

Extensive lands were also given to the missions of Espíritu Santo and Rosario after they were established in 1749 and 1754, respectively. Under a grant made in 1759, Espíritu Santo owned more land and cattle than any other mission or individual in Texas in the eighteenth century. Although it claimed land that went "from the sea to the sources of the Guadalupe," its pasture were generally considered to lie in the fork between the San Antonio and Guadalupe rivers, bound on the north by a line running from the Paso de la Laja (Rock Shelf Ford, near present Kosciusko in Wilson County) to El Capote (Capote Hills near present Belmont in Gonzales County). Similarly, the pastures of Rosario extended from the Texas coast northward along the west side of the San Antonio River as far as Cíbolo junction.[21]

Interspersed within the mission lands were ranches granted to soldiers of the northern conquest and to Canary Islanders. From time to time, soldiers and private citizens (*vecinos*) petitioned the king for grants of land, and the monarch often responded by generously awarding them some of the vacant and unappropriated land that was formerly given to the missions.

The first of these private land grants was that awarded jointly to Andrés Hernández and Luís Antonio Menchaca. Scions of soldiers of the Alarcón expedition that founded San Antonio de Béxar in 1718, these two men effected a "compromise donation" dated April 12, 1758, that alluded to earlier grants to the same parties. Hernández received the eastern portion of the wedge of land called El Rincón (The Corner) between

20. Cf. Title to the Land Grants Made to the Missions of San Antonio, Spanish Archives of the General Land Office, Austin, Texas.

21. Charles Ramsdell, Jr., "Spanish Goliad," (Typescript, State Parks Report, 1934, Records of the National Parks Service, University of Texas Library, Austin).

the San Antonio River and Arroyo de Cíbolo, and Menchaca received the western part. Hernandez called his ranch *San Bartolomé*. Situated on the west bank of Cibolo Creek near present Panna Maria, Czestochowa, and Kosciusko, it consisted of four leagues and eight *caballerías,* or 18,599 acres. Menchaca called his ranch *San Francisco,* which lay on the east bank of the San Antonio River between present Floresville and Falls City and consisted of eleven leagues and four *caballerías,* or 49,107 acres of land. Between *San Bartolomé* (sometimes called *San Bartolo*) and *San Francisco* was a ranch deeded to the Indians of Mission San Juan Capistrano called *Pataguilla.* [22]

About 1760, various other citizens of San Antonio and La Bahía began to establish ranches along the San Antonio River and Arroyo del Cíbolo for the purpose of raising *ganados mayores* (large stock: cattle, horses, donkeys, and mules) and *ganados menores* (small stock: sheep and goats). By the time of the American Revolution, ranching between Béxar and La Bahía had reached astonishing proportions. Thousands of head of livestock roamed the ranges that belonged to the missions and citizens.

As was the custom of the time, ranches were usually given descriptive nicknames. Extant land titles, survey field notes, and various other records identify in this region, besides *San Bartolomé, San Francisco,* and *Pataguilla,* the following ranches in operation during the period of the American Revolution:

> *Rancho de la Mora,* which belonged to the Mission
> San Antonio de Valero
> *Rancho de Laguna de las Animas,* which belonged to
> Manuel Delgado
> *Rancho de las Cabras,* which belonged to Mission San
> Francisco de la Espada
> *Rancho del Paso de las Mujeras,* which belonged to
> Ignacio Calvillo

22. Compromise Donation Between Luís Antonio Menchaca and Andrés Hernández, April 12, 1758 (Spanish Archives of the General Land Office, Austin, Texas).

Rancho de los Chayopínes, which belonged to Francisco Flores de Ábrego

Rancho de San Rafael, which belonged to Simón and Juan de Arocha

Rancho del Paistle, which belonged to Mission Concepción

Rancho de las Mulas, which belonged to Vizente Álvarez Travieso and his sons, Tomás and Francisco

Rancho de San José de los Alamos, which was operated by Doña Leonora Delgado, widow of Juan José Flores, who died on January 19, 1779

Rancho de Nuestra Señora de la Candelaria de las Calaveras, which belonged to Macario Zambrano

Rancho de Santa Cruz de la Laja, which was operated by Diego Yrineo Rodríguez

Rancho de San Lorenzo de las Mulas, which was operated by María Robaina de Betancourt, widow of Lorenzo de Armas

Rancho de San Cristóbal de Espanta Perros, which was operated by Manuel Delgado

Rancho de San Antonio del Cíbolo, which was operated by Maria Robaina de Betancourt

Rancho de Palo Quemado, which was also operated by María Robaina de Betancourt

Rancho de San Miguel de Amoladeras, which was operated by Miguel Guerra

Rancho de San Yldefonso de Chayopín, which was operated by Joseph Ygnacio de la Peña

Rancho del Capitán, which formerly belonged to Captain Manuel Ramírez y Piscina and was now operated by Mission Rosario

Rancho de Señor San José, which belonged to Carlos Martínez

Rancho del Diesmero, which was rented from Mission Rosario by Juan Barrera

15

Rancho de las Hermanas, which was owned by
   Andrés Benites Courbiere
Rancho de Gertrúdis Rodríguez, which was operated
   by Tomás Travieso
Rancho del Atascoso, which belonged to Mission San
   José
Rancho de San Lucas, which was owned by Domingo
   Castelo[23]

A number of nondescript ranches also were situated along the streams near Béxar. Included were the ranches belonging to Joseph Martín de la Garza, Juachín de la Garza, Luís Pérez, Juan Manuel Pérez, Juan Manuel Ruíz, Francisco Xavier Rodríguez, Juan Ignacio Pérez, Miguel Gortari, and the ranches belonging to the families of Leal, Micheli, Navarro, and Herrera.[24]

Spanish records for the period contain the names of the many cattlemen in the Béxar-La Bahía region. As will be pointed out a little later, many of these ranchers, and their vaqueros, lent a hand in the winning of the American Revolution. A roll call of these ranchers, compiled from several sources, would include the following names:

Chepe Arocha
Estanislao Arocha
Juan de Arocha
Julián de Arocha
Simón de Arocha
Blás de Ávila

Juan Bueno

Ignacio Calvillo
Joseph Pérez Casanova
Manuel Casanova
Marcos de Castro
Joseph Antonio Curbelo

Clemente Delgado
Jazinto Delgado
Manuel Delgado
Torivio Durán

Cano Flores
Francisco Flores de Ábrego
Jose Francisco Flores
Joseph Juachín Flores
Juan Joseph Flores
Vizente Flores

23. These ranches are located, identified, and described in Weddle and Thonhoff, *Drama & Conflict: The Texas Saga of 1776,* 144-159.
   24. *Ibid.*

16

Joseph Martín de la Garza
Juachín de la Garza
Leonardo de la Garza
Miguel de la Garza
Miguel de Gortari
Pedro Granados
Francisco Guerra
Mariano Guerra
Miguel Guerra

Francisco Hernández
Joseph Andres Hernández
Joseph Placido Hernández

Juachín Leal

Carlos Martínez
Luciano Martínez
Joseph Félix Menchaca
Juachín Menchaca
Luís Antonio Menchaca
Sebastián Monjarás
Joseph María Móntes
Marcos Móntes

Manuel Padrón
Joseph Ignacio de la Peña
Juan Ignacio Pérez

Cayetano Rentería
Carlos Riójas
Francisco Rodríguez
Francisco Xaviér Rodríguez

Pedro Xaviér Salinas
José Sánches
Joseph Antonio Saucedo
Santiago Seguín
Joseph de Sosa
Manuel de Soto

Chico Travieso
Francisco Travieso
Juan Andrés Travieso
Tomás Travieso
Vizente Álvarez Travieso

Joseph Macario Zambrano
Marcos Zepeda
Joseph Francisco de la Zerda[25]

25. This list of Béxar ranchers was compiled from the following sources: Petition of Cíbolo Ranchers, October 5, 1778 (Spanish Archives of the General Land Office); List of Citizens Who Are Going Out to Their Ranchos to Get their Cattle, July 14, 1781, Bexar Archives; Record of the Persons Who Went to the Roundup and Who Took Unbranded Cattle from the Pastures of the Ranchos of Las Mulas and San Bartolo, April 28, 1781, Bexar Archives; and Record Made by Don Macario Zambrano of the Number of *Orejana* Cattle and Mustang Horses Caught by Residents of the Said Villa and by Persons from the Presidio of San Antonio de Béxar in the Roundup Which Was Done to Gather Cattle and Proceed with Branding, December 23, 1782, Bexar Archives.

A composite of the picture of Texas in 1779, therefore, would look something like this: About three thousand people lived in and around the settlements at Béxar, La Bahía, and Nacogdoches. There were five active missions near Béxar and two at La Bahía. About one hundred men were on duty at Presidio San Antonio de Béxar, and about sixty men were stationed at Presidio La Bahía. Between these two presidios was the outpost of El Fuerte del Cíbolo, where twenty men from Béxar were detached to guard the many ranches in the area. And on these ranches grazed great numbers of branded and unbranded cattle—Texas Longhorns that provided the direct link between Texas and the American Revolution.

II

THE SPANISH PARTICIPATION

Riveting both ends of the Texas link to the American Revolution was Bernardo de Gálvez, truly a great figure of the time. Once the facts of his meteoric and heroic career become sufficiently understood by Americans, his name will rightfully rank with those of Lafayette, de Grasse, and Rochambeau of France; of von Steuben and de Kalb of Prussia; and of Pulaski and Kosciusko of Poland. As Spanish governor of the Province of Louisiana, Gálvez, in addition to supplying American forces with great amounts of money and supplies, militarily defeated the British along the entire Gulf Coast of North America. Yet, for some reason or reasons, he has been given very little recognition.

Bernardo de Gálvez was born in the village of Macharaviaya in the Province of Malaga, Spain, on July 23, 1746. He was the first son of Matías de Gálvez and Josefa Gallardo, both of ancient nobility. He belonged to a family that during his lifetime was one of the most distinguished in the royal service of Spain. His father, Matías de Gálvez, after serving as Captain-General of Guatemala, was elevated to Viceroy of New Spain (1783-1784). His uncle, José de Gálvez, a former *visitador* to New Spain who became Minister of the Indies, exercised power second only to King Carlos III himself. Another uncle, Miguel de Gálvez, was a field marshal in the royal army. A third uncle,

Antonio de Gálvez, served as an ambassador to the czar of Russia.[1]

Following a family tradition, Bernardo chose a military career in the service of his king. In 1762, when he was but sixteen years old, he served as lieutenant in a war with Portugal, after which he was promoted to captain in the Regiment of Corruna. He arrived in Mexico for the first time in 1765 as a part of his Uncle José's *entourage* for the visitation of the viceroyalty of New Spain. In 1769 he was commissioned by Viceroy Croix to go to the northern frontier on New Spain and be second in command under Lope de Cuellar, commandant of the army of Nueva Vizcaya. On April 11th of that year he was named captain of an expedition against the Apaches on the frontier. Shortly thereafter, Gálvez was named as successor to Cuellar.[2]

As commandant of this northern frontier province, Gálvez personally led several major expeditions against the Apaches, whose depredations seriously crippled the economy of the region. On the first of these, in October, 1770, he amply demonstrated the qualities of leadership that he possessed. With a company of about one hundred and thirty-five men, he set out from Chihuahua and headed northeastward in search of the enemy Indians. By the time they located the elusive Apaches at the Pecos River, their supplies had run short, and the men were suffering from cold and hunger, and prudence seem to dictate an immediate return to Chihuahua. Undaunted by adversity, young Bernardo made a stirring pep talk to his men, who unanimously chose to follow their leader and complete their mission. That November 2nd, they attacked the Indians, killing twenty-eight, capturing thirty-six, and taking 204 horses and two thousand *pesos'* worth of buffalo and antelope hides. Gálvez, setting an example which his soldiers followed, plunged

1. Guillermo Porras Muñoz, *Bernardo de Gálvez* (Madrid, 1952), 6-7. There seems to be a variation in the birthdate of Bernardo de Gálvez, which will have to be proved. Some authorities such as Muñoz gives July 23, 1746; other publications, such as *Ya* (Madrid, Spain newspaper, July 4, 1976) show July 25, 1746.

2. *Ibid.*; John Walton Caughey, *Bernardo de Gálvez in Louisiana, 1776-1783* (Reprint, Gretna, Louisiana, 1972), 61-62.

BERNARDO de GÁLVEZ

his horse into the stream to attack escaping Indians in the water, "where they perished between the two elements."[3]

This was Gálvez's initiation in frontier warfare, and it provided him with valuable experience for successive campaigns. Viceroy Croix commended the "glorious action" of young Gálvez to royal authorities in Spain. Six months later, after a second successful expedition against the Apaches, Croix recommended his promotion to lieutenant colonel, which was shortly approved. In October 1771, while on his way by himself to join a group of soldiers, he encountered five enemy Indians, and in a single-handed fight he dispersed them but was left with a wound in the arm by an arrow and a wound in the chest by two lance thrusts.[4]

In November of the same year, he made his last campaign against the Apaches in the Gila River region. Still convalescing from his wounds, he was thrown from his horse and received further injury to his chest. In the meantime, however, the *visitador-general* had asked that his nephew be relieved of duty in Nueva Vizcaya and be allowed to return with him to Spain. Accordingly, Hugo Oconór, former *ad interim* governor of Texas, was sent to take his place. Oconór arrived in Chihuahua in December while Gálvez was still off on his last Indian campaign. Gálvez returned to Mexico City in February, escorting fourteen captive Apache Indians, whom he enrolled in the *Colegio de San Gregorio*. Then he joined his Uncle José de Gálvez in Veracruz, where they boarded a ship for return to Spain.[5]

By the middle of 1772, Gálvez recovered his health. Then he requested and received leave of absence to go to France and enroll in the Regiment of Cantabria to perfect himself in military science. He spent three years there and attained the rank of lieutenant in this illustrious organization. In 1775 he returned to Spain and was incorporated into the Regiment of

3. Caughey, *Bernardo de Gálvez in Louisiana, 1776-1783*, 62-64. This fight apparently took place at a crossing on the Pecos River that came to be designated as Paso de Gálvez (See Robert S. Weddle, *San Juan Bautista: Gateway to Texas*, 337-338).

4. *Ibid.*, 65-66.

5. *Ibid.*

Seville. As captain of the infantry under Alejandro O'Reilly, he participated in an ill-fated attack on Algiers and suffered another wound. In recompense, he was promoted to the rank of lieutenant colonel and attached to the Military School of Ávila, but a new destiny awaited him another time in America.[6]

In 1776 he was transferred to the faraway Province of Louisiana as colonel of the Louisiana Regiment. Hardly having time to familiarize himself with his new duties, he acquired new responsibilities by a royal order dated September 9, 1776, instructing him to succeed Luís de Unzaga as acting governor of the colony. On January 1, 1777, he took over the office.[7]

Many and varied were his new duties as governor. According to instructions sent to him by the Minister of the Indies, his Uncle José, in a letter dated November 25, 1776, Gálvez was required to make an annual census; to visit the provincial districts, including Natchitoches, Opelousas, and Attakapas, and to obtain full written accounts of the affairs at the posts beyond the Arkansas, giving special attention to the English frontier; to get maps of the Mississippi and the coast from Balize to Bahía del Espíritu Santo; to admit foreigners who were Catholics and would take the oath of allegiance to Spain; to adopt strong measures against illegal commerce; to curtail trade with foreign vessels; to encourage the raising of tobacco; to cultivate friendship with the Indians; to treat slaves humanely; to organize a better-trained militia; to report on the state of religion, salt mines, roads, woodworkers, and the circulation of foreign money. Finally, he was instructed to collect information about affairs in the English colonies and to send secret commissioners for that purpose.[8]

In the two and one-half years of his administration prior to Spain's entry into the war, Gálvez did all that he could to weaken the British in that quarter of the continent. The struggle that was going on between England and her American colonies

6. *Ibid.*, 67; Muñoz, *Bernardo de Gálvez*, 10.
7. Caughey, *Bernardo de Gálvez in Louisiana, 1776-1783*, 67.
8. *Ibid.*, 68-69.

was watched with intense interest by the new Governor of Louisiana and by the Spanish court, which sent Gálvez several orders to afford secret assistance to the insurgent Americans. Throughout the years in which he sought solutions for domestic problems, Gálvez rendered important though unostentatious aid to the patriots in the American Revolution. From the start, Spain had maintained a lively interest in the conflict, and Gálvez held a special admiration for the Americans.

A brisk exchange of correspondence between patriot leaders and the Governor of Louisiana started shortly after the signing of the Declaration of Independence. In August, 1776, George Gibson, a Virginian, accompanied by sixteen other Americans disguised as traders, came to New Orleans from Fort Pitt on a mission that was to prove of utmost importance to the cause of America throughout the Revolution. Captain Gibson was the bearer of a dispatch from General Charles Lee, second in command of the American army. The message was calculated to win the favor of Governor Unzaga, Gálvez's predecessor, and gain assistance from King Carlos III and his advisors. Lee wrote:

> It must be known Sir that these provinces wearied with being repressed, and having flattered themselves for a long time, but in vain, for a redress from their ills by means of prayers and remonstrances, have at length determined to break all intercourse with a country which thay had always regarded as their mother but which they can now no longer regard else than as a scourge of injustice and cruelty. They lack neither force nor courage to maintain their rights, but they do lack the means necessary to maintain war.[9]

In return for the "known generosity of the Spaniards," which Lee pleaded should be extended at that time, he set forth all the advantages that would come to Spain through trade with the thirteen United States. Specifically, Lee asked the Spanish

9. James Alton James, "Oliver Pollock, Financier of the Revolution in the West," *Mississippi Valley Historical Review* (1929), XVI, 67.

government to send the American army such necessities as guns, gunpowder, blankets, and medicine, especially quinine. Largely through the influence of Oliver Pollock, sometimes called "the Robert Morris of the West," Gibson was received favorably by Governor Unzaga. The following month 9000 pounds of gunpowder were sent up the Mississippi River to American forces in Virginia. Another 1000 pounds were sent by sea to Philadelphia.[10]

In January, 1777, Unzaga introduced Pollock to his successor, Bernardo de Gálvez, as a "faithful and zealous American in whom he might impose implicit confidence." Gálvez at once assured Pollock that he would give all possible aid to the Americans. He declared that the port of New Orleans would be open and free to American commerce and to the admission and sale of prizes made by American cruisers. American trading vessels, upon arrival at the mouth of the river, were to be seized as Spanish property in order to protect them from British sloops and then later released.[11]

More aid to American forces in goods and money was forthcoming. By July, 1777, 2000 barrels of gunpowder, a quantity of lead, and a large amount of clothing were sent up the Mississippi. King Carlos III had even advanced a secret loan of 1,000,000 *livres* to the Americans. By the end of 1777, Gálvez had aided the Americans by sending great amounts of arms, ammunition, and provisions to the Mississippi posts of George Rogers Clark and to the Pennsylvania and Virginia arenas of George Washington's Continental Army.[12]

Patrick Henry, Governor of Virginia, wrote two letters in October, 1777, and a third one in January, 1778, to Gálvez. In them he asked for more military supplies and proposed the idea that Spain regain the two Floridas (East Florida and West Florida) that she lost to England in 1763, an idea that fell into fertile ground. In a letter dated May 6, 1778, Galvez replied to Henry, acknowledging Henry's appreciation for the cordial

10. *Ibid.*, 67-70.
11. *Ibid.*, 71.
12. *Ibid.*, 72.

reception given to Captain Gibson and for the stock of goods that were furnished at that time. Gálvez concluded the letter by assuring Henry that he would not spare any effort or trouble which may redound to the benefit of the colonies, on account of the particular affection he had for them.[13] In a letter to Gálvez on November 8, 1779, even Thomas Jefferson expressed appreciation for Spanish aid.[14]

The highlight of Gálvez's pro-American activities came in 1778, when he welcomed the bizarre expedition of Captain James Willing to New Orleans. In March, 1778, Willing arrived in New Orleans at the head of a strange assortment of boats, including his own *Rattletrap*. In one of the least known and most spectacular raids of the American Revolution, Willing had set out from Fort Pitt with a volunteer crew of about thirty men. His mission was to bear dispatches to New Orleans, convey supplies back north, solicit the support or neutrality of West Florida, and confiscate British property along the way, to be sold in New Orleans to provide funds for the Revolution. On the way down the Ohio and Mississippi rivers, Willing and his men raided and burned British holdings on the east bank of the river, captured slaves and other properties, including boats and barges of plantation owners, and one armed British ship. By the time they reached New Orleans, their number had swelled to nearly 150 men. Governor Gálvez welcomed them, gave them freedom of the city, provided quarters, allowed them to sell their loot at public auction, and then sold them military supplies for their return trip.[15]

In his campaign against the British at Kaskaskia, Cahokia, and Vincennes in 1778-1779, George Rogers Clark received a

13. Cf., Letters from Henry to Gálvez in Lawrence Kinnaird (Ed.), *Spain in the Mississippi Valley, 1765-1794* (Annual Report of the American Historical Association, Washington, D.C., 1949), II, 241-242, 248-250; and Gálvez to Henry, II, 272-273.

14. *Ibid.*, II, 362-364.

15. *Texas and the American Revolution* (Institute of Texan Cultures at San Antonio, 1976), 15-17; cf. Caughey, *Bernardo de Gálvez* in Louisiana, 1776-1783, 102-134 for the most extensive treatment of the Willing expedition.

considerable part of his supplies from New Orleans by way of the Mississippi. In these important operations, one man stands out as Clark's main support. That man was Oliver Pollock, a wealthy merchant of New Orleans, who served Clark in much the same way that Robert Morris, "The Financier of the Revolution," served Washington. Pollock, at New Orleans, with the blessings of Gálvez, was the "good angel" of the Clark campaigns in the Northwest. Not only did he furnish essential supplies by way of the Mississippi, but he contributed what was equally important—credit—in excess of $300,000.[16]

Thus it can be clearly seen, that prior to Spain's official entry into the war, she gave considerably more than moral support. Secured by Gálvez, the Mississippi River served as a veritable lifeline to American forces, and the amount of men, money, supplies, and correspondence that moved up and down it were considerably greater than most people realize.

Spain formally declared war against Great Britain, on the side of the American colonies, on May 8, 1779. Tacit support could now be open and direct. After Willing's expedition, the English posts at Manchac, Baton Rouge, and Natchez along the lower Mississippi were enlarged and improved. Anticipating the declaration of war, which did not reach him till August, Gálvez wasted no time in making military preparations. Even when he did receive notice of the declaration of war, he made no public announcement but kept the news secret. In the meantime, supplies were collected, and men were recruited "for the defense of Louisiana."[17]

His strategy resembled that which Clark had employed in his attack on Hamilton at Vincennes—a swift blow at the nearest stronghold, which in this case would be Fort Bute at Manchac, about ninety miles up the river from New Orleans. Under the pretense of preparing for "the defense of New Orleans," Gálvez prepared for a campaign against the British installations along the east bank of the lower Mississippi. When

16. James G. Randall, "George Rogers Clark's Service of Supply," *The Mississippi Valley Historical Review* (December, 1921), 251-261.

17. Caughey, *Bernardo de Gálvez in Louisiana, 1776-1783*, 149-153.

he received notice of the declaration of war in August, he kept it secret, along with the news that he had been appointed Governor of Louisiana; up to that time he had been acting governor. He convened a council of war and proposed a march against the British at Fort Bute on August 23rd. He planned to make an appeal for public support three days previous to departure, but on the 18th, a hurricane, a well-known visitor of the country, delayed his planned speech and departure a few more days.[18]

On August 27th the little army set out. It was composed of 170 veteran soldiers, 330 recruits newly arrived from Mexico and the Canary Islands, 20 carabineers, 60 militiamen, 80 free blacks and mulattoes, and 7 American volunteers. Among the latter was Oliver Pollock, agent of Virginia and the Continental Congress, who served as aide-de-camp to Gálvez throughout the war. The force totalled 667 men. A flotilla of four vessels under command of Juan Álvarez was to go up the river while Gálvez led the land expedition. They had to march through thick woods and over difficult trails. On the way, Gálvez enlisted another 600 men from the German and Acadian coasts and 160 Indians, giving him a force of 1427 men. The difficult journey of thirty-five leagues (one league equals 2.63 statute miles) was made in eleven days. Only when they had come into sight of Fort Bute at Manchac on September 6th did Gálvez announce to his men that Spain had declared war against Great Britain and that he was ordered to attack their posts on the Mississippi.[19]

Reasoning that Manchac could not be defended against an attack, British Lieutenant Colonel Alexander Dickson had already withdrawn most of his men to a new fortification at Baton Rouge. A few men, however, were still at Fort Bute, and Gálvez had first to capture it. On the night of the 6th, the Spanish forces took position around the fort. The next morning the assault was made. One British soldier was killed, two officers and eighteen soldiers were taken prisoner, and one officer and five soldiers escaped. There were no Spanish losses. Although

18. *Ibid.*
19. *Ibid.*, 154-155; Charles Gayarré, *Hsitory of Louisiana* (4 vols., New Orleans, 1879), III, 126-127.

not a great military exploit, it was a good initiation for Gálvez's troops, who were greatly heartened by their victory.[20]

On September 8th, an inventory of the fort was made, and the next six days were spent resting and preparing for a march on Baton Rouge. A contingent of men under Carlos Grand Pré had already been sent to occupy a position between Baton Rouge and Natchez to interrupt communications. While there, they captured two English posts, one on the Amite River and the other on Thompson's Creek, whose garrisons became prisoners of war. In the meantime, Gálvez's troops advanced to a point a mile and a half from Baton Rouge, where the artillery was landed from the boats and the army made its quarters.[21]

The fort at Baton Rouge was much more formidable than the one at Manchac. Garrisoned by four hundred regulars and one hundred fifty militiamen, the fort was protected by high palisade walls and was surrounded by a ditch eighteen feet wide and nine feet deep. It had eighteen cannons, whereas Gálvez had only ten. So Gálvez had to devise different tactics than the kind used at Manchac.[22]

A small grove of trees projecting outward from the fort appeared to be the best place from which to attack. On the night of September 20th, Gálvez sent a large detachment to chop down trees, throw up earthworks, fire on the fort, and generally make as much noise as possible. The ruse worked. While the English concentrated on bombarding the grove all night, the Spaniards were placing their cannon, unmolested and unobserved, in a garden on the opposite side of the fort, within musket shot range. In the morning the English discovered their mistake and directed their fire at the Spanish batteries. But it was too late. The well-sheltered Spanish batteries opened fire. By mid-afternoon the fort was so damaged that Colonel Dickson sent out two officers under a white flag to propose a truce. Gálvez insisted that Dickson surrender at discretion and that Fort Pan-

20. *Ibid.*

21. Gayarré, *History of Louisiana*, III, 127.

22. *Ibid.*, 128; Caughey, *Bernardo de Gálvez in Louisiana, 1776-1783*, 155-156.

mure, with its garrison of eighty men at Natchez, also be included. Dickson accepted the conditions, and after twenty-four hours granted to him to bury the dead, the British soldiers marched out with military honors the customary five hundred paces from the fort, where they delivered up their arms and flags, and became prisoners of war. Three hundred seventy-five surviving British regulars were sent to New Orleans as prisoners of war. The enlisted settlers and negroes were parolled on the spot by Gálvez.[23]

Captain Juan de la Villebeuvre was dispatched with fifty soldiers to receive the surrender of Fort Panmure at Natchez. With letters from Dickson and Pollock, he secured the peaceful surrender of the fort and its garrison on October 5th.[24]

While Gálvez was metting with success after success, an American schooner commanded by William Pickles boarded and captured the English privateer *West Florida,* which had dominated Lake Pontchartrain for two years. Other prizes were taken by the Spanish near Galveztown, a new-found settlement of Canary Islanders at Bayou Manchac, named in honor of Gálvez.[25]

In less than a month, Gálvez and his forces had achieved signal success. Three forts had been captured, one by assault, one by bombardment, the third by cession. Five hundred fifty regular soldiers had been taken prisoner, and more than five hundred settlers and negroes taken with arms were parolled on their honor not to take up arms against the Spanish again. Gálvez kept more than five hundred prisoners in New Orleans, and only fifty Spanish soldiers were needed to guard them. The English soldiers did not violate the parole that gave them the freedom of the town.[26]

Gálvez's success in the capture of Manchac, Baton Rouge,

23. Caughey, *Bernardo de Gálvez in Louisiana, 1776-1783,* 156-157.
24. *Ibid.,* 157-159.
25. *Ibid.,* 159-161.
26. Gayarré, *History of Louisiana,* III, 132-133.

and Natchez brought him a promotion to brigadier-general. At the same time, his capture of these English forts on the lower Mississippi caused great consternation in other British establishments in the Floridas.[27]

With official notice of the rupture between Spain and England, Gálvez had received instructions "to drive the British forces out of Pensacola, Mobile, and other posts they occupy on the Mississippi.[28] A royal order dated August 29, 1779, defined the Spanish objective thusly:

> The king has determined that the principal object of his forces in America during the war against the English shall be to expel them from the Gulf of Mexico and the banks of the Mississippi where they establishments are so prejudicial to our commerce and also to the security of our more valuable possessions.[29]

Even before setting out for Manchac, Baton Rouge, and Natchez, Gálvez had begun to plan the conquest of Mobile and Pensacola. He called upon Jacinto Panis, who had visited the places the previous year, to prepare a plan for their seizure. Strengthened by his recent victories along the lower Mississippi, Gálvez was able, in the fall of 1779, to push forward his military preparations much more rapidly. With Panis and Juan Antonio Gayarré, his commissary of war, Gálvez spent the remainder of 1779 preparing for a spring offensive. Contrary to the advice of bureaucrats in Havana, he decided to concentrate first on the capture of Mobile as a vital stepping stone to the conquest of Pensacola, the British capital of West Florida.[30]

By January 11, 1780, his expeditionary force was ready to set out from New Orleans. On board a fleet of twelve ships were

27. Francois-Xavier Martin, *The History of Louisiana* (Reprint, New Orleans, 1963), 228.

28. Caughey, *Bernardo de Gálvez in Louisiana, 1776-1783*, 171.

29. *Ibid.*

30. Gayarré, *History of Louisiana*, III, 135.

a total of 754 men comprised of 43 men of the Regiment of Principe of the Second Battalion of Spain, 50 of the fixed Regiment of Havana, 141 of the fixed Regiment of Louisiana, 14 artillerymen, 26 carabineers, 323 white militiamen, 107 free blacks and mulattoes, 24 slaves, and 26 Anglo-American auxiliaries. They were to rendezvous with another 1412 men to be sent from Havana. By January 28th, the ships descended the Mississippi to its mouth and sailed out into the Gulf. Beset alternately by calms and storms, they finally reached the entrance to Mobile Bay on February 10th. The next few days, amidst many difficulties, Gálvez landed his troops.[31]

Gálvez immediately established a battery on Mobile Point to command the entrance to the bay. The rest of the men were then moved up the bay toward Mobile. On February 20th, the convoy and ships transporting 1412 reinforcements and supplies from Havana arrived. Gálvez's forces now numbered over two thousand men.[32]

Under the cover of naval barrage, Gálvez's troops moved to a new camp just two thousand varas from Fort Charlotte. On February 29th, the British welcomed a scouting party of four companies with cannon balls and grapeshot. On March 1st, Gálvez began a chivalrous correspondence with Captain Elias Durnford, commander of Fort Charlotte, demanding surrender. The exchange lasted several days, with the British cordially declining. Between letters, Gálvez continued preparations for an attack on the fort. An intercepted letter revealed that a large force led by General John Campbell, commandant at Pensacola, was on its way to help Durnford. By March 9th Spanish preparations for the attack were complete. That night, in a manner reminiscent of his Texas Apache campaign, Gálvez made a short pep talk. After the speech, five hundred soldiers, under the dark and quiet of night, left camp to open a trench for artillery

31. *Caughey, Bernardo de Gálvez in Louisiana, 1776-1783,* 175-176; Jack D.L. Holmes, *Honor and Fidelity* (Birmingham, 1965), 32. In addition to a concise summary of Gálvez's activities during the American Revolution, Holmes' book has the service records for over 1500 men of the Louisiana military units, 1766-1821.

32. Kinnaird, *Spain in the Mississippi Valley,* II, 368-370.

emplacements within musket shot range of the fort. The next morning it was detected by the British, who directed fire at it, killing six and wounding five Spaniards. Gálvez called off the work until nightfall, when it could be done again with less risk. After two more nights of work, by ten o'clock in the morning, the Spanish battery of eight eighteen pounders and one twenty-four pounder was completed and commenced firing. During the day the Spaniards lost one more dead and three wounded. At sundown the British sent out a white flag of truce asking for a cease-fire until terms of surrender might be arranged. Gálvez agreed, on condition that Durnford promise not to make delays in hope of receiving reinforcements from Pensacola (that had turned back) or allowing sailors and civilians who assisted in the defense of the fort to leave. On March 13th, the terms of capitulation were agreed upon, and on the 14th the Spaniards took possession of the fort.[33]

As reward for the capture of Mobile, Gálvez was promoted to the rank of *mariscal de campo,* or field marshal, and he was given command of all Spanish operations in America.[34]

The stage was now set for the principal objective of the Gulf Coast campaign: the conquest of Pensacola, the capital of British West Florida. After the surrender of Mobile, Gálvez wanted to attack Pensacola immediately, before General Campbell had a chance to shore up his defenses. But two expected convoys with reinforcements from Havana failed to arrive, and the attack had to be postponed.[35]

Bureaucratic authorities in Havana continued to drag their feet, and Gálvez, impatient with their inaction and further delay, decided to go to Havana himself and push through matters personally. A garrison was left at Mobile under Colonel Joseph Ezpeleta, and the greater part of the Spanish forces were returned to Havana and New Orleans. The summer months were spent by Gálvez personally prodding governmental and

---

33. Caughey, *Bernardo de Gálvez in Louisiana, 1776-1783,* 177-181.
34. *Ibid.,* 186.
35. *Ibid.,* 187-191.

military authorities into action for an attack against Pensacola that fall.[36]

Gálvez succeeded in his efforts, and elaborate preparations were made for the expedition that finally set sail for Pensacola on October 16, 1780. It consisted of a fleet of seven warships, five frigates, one packet, one brig, one armed lugger, and forty-nine transports carrying a landing force of 164 officers and 3829 men. But bad luck struck again. Two days out of Havana, the fleet was hit by a hurricane. One ship was sunk, several were crippled, and others were hopelessly scattered, from the Gulf Coast to Yucatan. After a fruitless effort to reunite his fleet, Gálvez returned to Havana on November 16th, one month after he had set out.[37]

Spared again from attack, the British decided to recover Mobile. Gálvez worried about Mobile's exposure, and in December he sent Joseph Rada with two warships and four transports carrying five hundred men to reinforce Ezpeleta. But, unable to find safe passage into Mobile Bay, Rada delivered the convoy to New Orleans. Early in January, 1781, General Campbell sent a force of three hundred soldiers and three hundred Indians to seize Mobile. An assault on January 7th was successfully repulsed by the Spaniards, and the British retreated. Mobile was saved, but at the cost of fourteen Spanish soldiers killed and another twenty-three wounded.[38]

The British attack on Mobile and its gallant defense spurred Havana authorities to aid Gálvez more promptly. They agreed to provide him with another 1315 soldiers to strengthen his defenses on the mainland and authorized another expeditionary force to capture Pensacola. Gálvez's strategy this time was to invest the British stronghold both by land and sea. On February 28th a vanguard fleet of one man-of-war, three frigates, one packet, and several transports carrying troops and supplies left Havana for Pensacola. More troops would come later, and supply ships would leave at fifteen-day intervals.

36. *Ibid.,* 191-193.
37. *Ibid.,* 193.
38. *Ibid.,* 194-195.

Commanding the fleet was Joseph Calvo de Irazabal. Colonel Pedro Piernas was ordered to mobilize Louisiana forces at New Orleans and transport them by sea to join with the Havana forces at Pensacola. On March 1st, Gálvez sent orders to Colonel Ezpeleta to march overland from Mobile to Pensacola with as many troops as possible.[39]

The two-month-long siege of Pensacola began on March 9th, when Gálvez, under the cover of dark, landed his troops, ordnance, and military stores on Santa Rosa Island, which fronted Pensacola Bay. Early the next morning, a detachment was sent to capture the redoubt at Sigüenza Point, which was found already abandoned. Shortly after daybreak, seven Englishmen came to shore in two rowboats from an English frigate to tend to some cattle on the island. They were surprised and taken prisoner, whereupon the Spaniards were also discovered, and a lively but harmless bombardment was commenced by two British frigates in the bay and by nearby Fort Barrancas Coloradas. A battery erected by Gálvez's men returned fire and forced the two frigates to withdraw out of range.[40]

On March 11th, Gálvez ordered the fleet to enter the bay, but Admiral Calvo, who was independent of Gálvez, refused to allow the ships to cross the shallow bar under the guns of Fort Barrancas Coloradas, alleging that to do so would invite certain destruction. Inclement weather then compounded an already difficult situation, and Gálvez, fearing that the fleet might have to sail back to Havana and leave his troops marooned without adequate provisions, ordered the landing of all supplies on Santa Rosa Island. Then he ordered the emplacement of more artillery and the reconnaissance of the island.[41]

---

39. *Ibid.*, 198-200.

40. *Ibid.*, 201-202; and Diary of the Operations of the Expedition Against the Place Pensacola, Concluded by the Arms of H. Catholic M., Under the Orders of Field Marshal Don Bernardo de Gálvez (translated by Gaspar Cusachs), *Louisiana Historical Quarterly*, (January, 1917), I, 48-49 (hereafter cited as Diary . . . Bernardo de Gálvez).

41. Diary . . . Bernardo de Gálvez, 49-51.

Although Gálvez had been named commander of all naval and military operations in America, Calvo was responsible for the fleet's safety, and he continued his refusal to enter the bay. Unable to persuade or coerce him otherwise, Gálvez decided to shame him into compliance by running the gauntlet himself. Realizing that the success of the whole operation hinged upon the entrance of the fleet into the bay, Gálvez resorted to extraordinary and dramatic measures. On the morning of March 18th, he boarded the *Gálveztown*, ran up a big rear-admiral's ensign, ordered a departing fifteen-gun salute, and set sail. Followed by two armed launches and a sloop, these Louisiana vessels being the only ones under his private command, the *Gálveztown* crossed the bar and entered the channel. Fort Barrancas Coloradas artillery opened fire upon the tiny fleet, but the cannon balls hit only the rigging and the sails. Soon the four ships were safely anchored under the shelter of the Spanish battery at Sigüenza Point, and amidst the enthusiastic cheers of Gálvez's troops, another fifteen-gun salute was fired. The next day, the rest of the squadron entered the bay.[42]

In the meantime, a sloop from Mobile commanded by Lieutenant Juan Riano had arrived with a letter notifying Gálvez that Colonel Ezpeleta with nine hundred soldiers had reached the Río Perdido, five leagues west of Pensacola. Gálvez ordered armed launches to go there to help the Mobile forces cross the river.[43]

By March 22nd, Ezpeleta and his men appeared on the inner shore of Pensacola Bay. Gálvez, with five hundred men, crossed over to meet them and allow them rest. The next day a convoy of sixteen vessels carrying another 1400 men arrived from New Orleans. These additions more than doubled the size of Gálvez's forces, now numbering over 3500 men under arms.[44]

While awaiting reinforcements from Mobile and New Orleans, Gálvez started a correspondence with the British com-

42. *Ibid.*, 52; Caughey, *Bernardo de Gálvez in Louisiana, 1776-1783*, 202-203.

43. Diary . . . Bernardo de Gálvez, 51.

44. *Ibid.*, 56-58.

mander of Fort George, General John Campbell, and the British governor ot West Florida, Peter Chester. The intermediary was Colonel Alexander Dickson, who was taken prisoner at Baton Rouge and now resided in Pensacola under parole. For the most part, the exchange of letters concerned humanitarian considerations.[45]

Actual military operations against Fort George could now begin. On March 24th the remaining Spanish troops were ferried from Santa Rosa Island to the mainland. The forces spent the rest of March securing their siege and preparing for the battle that was sure to come. The only Spanish casualties were those caused by the Indian allies of the British.[46]

The Spaniards familiarized themselves thoroughly with all the approaches to the British fortifications, but they purposely avoided pitched battle. Occasionally British soldiers would fire upon Spaniards who came too near their lines, and the English came out a couple of times in sorties to drive back the Spaniards. During one of these encounters, on April 12th, Gálvez had a bullet go through a finger of his left hand and furrow his abdomen. Surgeons repaired the damage, and while Gálvez recuperated, Colonel Ezpeleta was placed in command.[47]

During the next few days, construction continued on fascines, artillery emplacements, and powder magazines. On the 18th, a brig from Havana brought the welcome news that Spanish forces under Matías de Gálvez, father of Bernardo, had dislodged British troops from the Castle of Nicaragua. To celebrate this, the General ordered a triple salute by both the army and the navy.[48]

On April 19th, eighteen ships under the command of Joseph Solano arrived from Havana with 1600 reinforcements under Field Marshal Juan Manuel Cagigal. Accompanying the Spanish force were four French frigates with 725 French soldiers aboard. Solano, in contrast to Calvo, showed great willingness to

45. *Ibid.*, 53-58.
46. Caughey, *Bernardo de Gálvez in Louisiana, 1776-1783*, 207.
47. Diary . . . Bernardo de Gálvez, 64-65.
48. *Ibid.*, 66.

cooperate with Gálvez in the campaign against Pensacola. He offered gunners, sailors, and two groups of soldiers, 1350 in all, which Gálvez gratefully accepted "in order that they also might share in the glory of this conquest." By April 23rd, approximately 3675 men were landed, increasing Gálvez's forces to more than 7000 men.[49]

The General ordered that the army be divided into four brigades. The first would be under command of Brigadier General Gerónimo Girón; the second under Colonel Manuel Pineda; the third under Colonel Francisco Longoria; and the fourth under Captain of the Ship Felipe López Carrizosa. The French division was placed under command of Captain of the Ship Mr. de Boiderout. Pensacola would be surrounded on land and sea by combined Spanish and French forces.[50]

Fort George, like the fort at Baton Rouge, was too strong to be taken by assault without great casualties. Therefore, Gálvez, after a month of scouting and planning, prepared for a heavy bombardment by land and sea. During the latter part of April, hundreds of men were detailed to dig a covered trench from Spanish lines to a small hill that could command a western redoubt called the Queen's Redoubt or "The Crescent," because of its semi-circular shape. On May 1st, a battery of six twenty-four pounders was set in place. The engineers extended the trench to other redoubt positions. Meantime, the British discovered the work, and each day was marked by cannon and mortar fire in the trench and redoubts. On May 4th, under the cover of barrage, the British infantry successfully assaulted a Spanish redoubt and then withdrew, capturing four Spanish officers and leaving behind eighteen killed and sixteen wounded soldiers.[51]

---

49. *Ibid.*, 66-67; One of the officers arriving with the expedition from Havana on April 19th was Francisco Miranda, who also kept a diary of the siege of Pensacola. Miranda arrived at the figure of 7803 effective troops under Gálvez. Cf. Donald E. Worcester (translator), "Miranda's Diary of the Siege of Pensacola, 1781," *The Florida State Historical Quarterly* (January, 1951), XXIX, 176.

50. Diary . . . Bernardo de Gálvez, 67.

51. *Ibid.*, 72-73.

Spanish bombardment commenced on the 6th, being answered in kind by the British. An assault on "The Crescent" was planned for the morning of the 7th, but an unexpected delay by some Spanish troops caused it to be called off. Artillery fire opened up again on the morning of May 8th, and a lucky shot from one of the Spanish batteries hit the powder magazine of "The Crescent." A great explosion followed, killing 105 British soldiers. Spanish troops under General Girón and Colonel Ezpeleta immediately advanced through a breach and took over the redoubt. So exposed was Fort George to bombardment and assault now that General Campbell, at three o'clock in the afternoon, ran up the white flag of surrender.[52]

Gálvez agreed to the truce and met with Campbell to work out the terms of surrender. At one o'clock the next morning both generals came to an agreement. On May 9th, the terms were set in writing, and on May 10th, at three o'clock in the afternoon, the British marched out five hundred yards from the fort and stacked their arms in customary ceremony, and Spanish troops took possession of the fort. On May 11th, a detachment was sent out to take possession of Fort Barrancas Coloradas.[53]

By Spanish count, the total number of prisoners taken was 1113. Add to that the 105 killed in "The Crescent," 56 deserters, and 300 who were allowed to return to Georgia during capitulation, and the total figure for the garrison reaches about 1600. Besides prisoners and many uncounted negroes who helped in the defense, there were also 101 women and 123 children. Spanish losses during the siege were 74 killed and 198 wounded. According to the articles of capitulation, the British soldiers were allowed to keep their personal property and to embark on a British ship to any British port excepting St. Augustine or in Jamaica, under promise that they would never take up arms against Spain unless officially exchanged.[54]

Gálvez's great feat at Pensacola was appreciated and commemorated by King Carlos III, who added to his titles that of

52. *Ibid.*, 73-74.
53. *Ibid.*, 74-75.
54. *Ibid.*, 75.

Count of Gálvez and Viscount of Gálveztown, with a special coat of arms emblazoned with the brig *Gálveztown* and the proud inscription of "Yo Solo" (I Alone). Further, he was promoted to the rank of lieutenant general and was commissioned as the governor of West Florida as well as Louisiana.[55]

After the capture of Pensacola, Gálvez was ordered to go to Santo Domingo to plan a joint venture with the French to conquer Jamaica. Francisco Miranda, who was an aide-de camp to Gálvez at Pensacola and who later achieved fame as the precursor of Latin American independence, was sent on a spying mission to Jamaica. But, even though plans were made, troops were mobilized, and ships and military stores were assembled, a series of difficulties caused the attack on Jamaica to miscarry.[56]

Though balked in this major effort, Gálvez supervised another important project, the conquest of the Bahamas, long a base for British privateers. In January, 1782, an army was mobilized under General Cagigal. After a three-month delay by naval authorities, Cagigal's expedition sailed out from Havana on April 22nd. Arriving at New Providence, the capital of the Bahamas, on May 6th, Cagigal sent word to British Governor John Maxwell to surrender in twelve hours or else. Maxwell complied, and the next day the terms of surrender were arranged through Cagigal's aide-de-camp, Francisco Miranda. They were signed on May 8th, with Maxwell surrendering his entire force and turning over to the Spaniards all the Bahama Islands. Besides a population of over three thousand persons, the Bahamas had a garrison of 274 regulars and 338 militiamen, with an inventory of military supplies that included 199 cannon, 868 muskets, and 41 hundredweight of gunpowder, besides balls and shells. Most important, however, was the capture of 12 privateers and 65 merchant vessels, which, during the war, had made prizes of 14 Spanish, 24 French, 1 Dutch, and 137 American vessels.[57]

Gálvez and his advisors contemplated other military actions

55. Caughey, *Bernardo de Gálvez in Louisiana, 1776-1783*, 213-214.
56. *Ibid.*, 243-244.
57. *Ibid.*, 245-246.

GOLFO DE MEXICO

VISTA DE
PANZACOLA
Y SV BAIA
Tomada por los Españoles
año de 1781.

1. Casa del Gobernador
2. Los Almacenes
3. Los Fosos
4. Fuerte de Sⁿ Carlos
5. Fuerte de Sᵗª Rosa
6. Bahia de Panzacola
7. Canal de Santa Rosa
8. Ysla de Sᵗª Rosa
9. Punta del Desembarco
10. Rio de la Vigia
11. La Iglesia
12. Trincheras de los Españoles
13. Desembarco
14. Tropa Española
15. Tropa Inglesa y el fuerte Jorge
16. El Castillo bolado de moda Luna.
Se Hallaran Madrid en la Librería
de la Viuda de Miguel Escribano
Calle de Corredas Nᵒ 8
Con el Nuevo Gibraltar.

VISTA de Panzacola y Su Baiá.

in the closing months of the war, including attacks on St. Augustine and Halifax. But the armistice and peace negotiations early in 1783 prevented these as well as the proposed Jamaica campaign.[58]

Gálvez's military campaigns went far in determining certain provisions of the Peace Treaty of 1783. Great Britain recognized her loss of the Gulf Coast and ceded both East Florida and West Florida back to Spain. More significantly to us, they aided the American colonists immeasurably in the war effort, both by providing arms, ammunition, and supplies by way of the Mississippi River and by diverting British manpower that could have been used against the Continental Army.

Immediately after the cessation of hostilities, Gálvez returned to Spain and remained there from September, 1783, till October, 1784. Later in 1784, he returned to America, going first to Havana as captain-general of Cuba, while still retaining the governorship of Louisiana and the two Floridas. He was in Cuba only long enough to render some important assistance again to Oliver Pollock and to be cited by the United States Congress for his aid during the Revolution.[59]

Upon the death of Matías de Gálvez, Bernardo was sent to Mexico City to succeed his father as Viceroy of New Spain. He arrived at Veracruz on May 21, 1785, with his wife and three children. In Mexico, as in Louisiana, Gálvez attained great popularity. In the first year of his administration, he made a promising beginning, but death suddenly intervened. Early in the fall of 1786, during an epidemic, he was stricken with sickness and died on November 30th, at the age of 38.[60] Thus the meteoric and heroic career of a truly great man came to an untimely end.

58. *Ibid.*, 247.
59. *Ibid.*
60. *Ibid.*, 256-257; Muñoz, *Bernardo de Gálvez*, 40-49, which describes Gálvez's career as Viceroy of New Spain.

General Gálvez before Fort George.

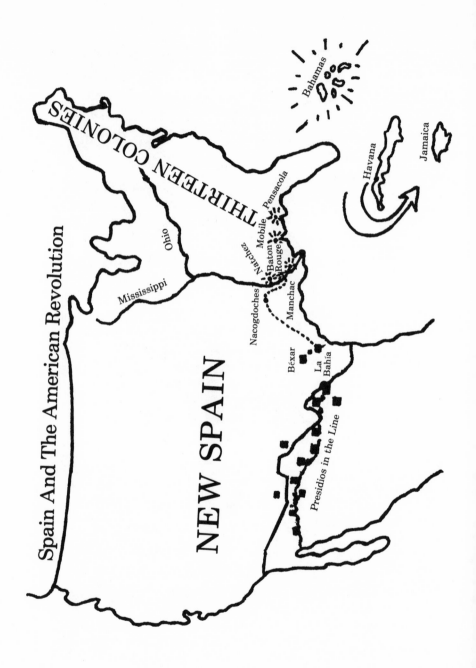

Spain And The American Revolution

THIRTEEN COLONIES

NEW SPAIN

Bahamas

Havana

Jamaica

Ohio

Mississippi

Pensacola

Mobile

Natchez

Baton Rouge

Nacogdoches

Manchac

Béxar

La Bahía

Presidios in the Line

III

THE TEXAS CONTRIBUTION

Texas Longhorn cattle provided the direct link between Texas and the American Revolution. People all over the world, thanks to Hollywood movies and television, know about the great Texas Longhorn cattle drives out of South Texas to the railheads in Kansas and elsewhere during the years following the Civil War. But mighty few people are aware of the fact that Texas Longhorns were trailed by Spanish Texans nearly a hundred years before the time usually ascribed to cattle drives. And although a few historians have known and written about the first drives of Texas cattle in 1779, only recently has their main purpose been discovered, which makes them doubly significant. Indeed, their story adds a new dimension to the history of the American Revolution. A more unique and interesting sidelight to the American Revolution could happen "Nowhere Else But Texas," where truth is often stranger than fiction.

Now for the story on "How the Texas Longhorns Helped Win American Independence"—

After the Battle of Saratoga, which we read about in school history books as being "the turning point of the American Revolution," the European countries of France, Spain, and Holland joined the American colonists in their fight against the British. After Spain declared war against Great Britain on May 8, 1779, King Carlos III commissioned Bernardo de Gálvez, whose exploits were described in the previous chapter, to raise and lead Spanish forces in a campaign against the British along the Gulf Coast. Accordingly, Gálvez proceeded to raise an army of 1400 men, which by 1781 had swelled to over 7000 men. Then, as now, the military axiom that "an army travels on its stomach" held true.

45

But Gálvez knew where the food supply was—better yet, he knew where there was a veritable travelling commissary for his troops! As a young lieutenant, it will be remembered, Gálvez was stationed in Chihuahua, where he led Spanish troops in a campaign against Apaches, once going as far as the Pecos River. While there, he learned of the great herds of cattle near Béxar in the Province of Texas. At that time, however, Texas cattle were prohibited from export to neighboring provinces and were worth only three or four pesos a head, valued only for their hides, tallow, or local consumption, which could not make a dent in their great numbers.

In order to feed his troops, Gálvez sent an emissary, Francisco García, with a letter to Texas Governor Domingo Cabello, both requesting and authorizing the very first official cattle drive out of Texas. García arrived in San Antonio de Béxar on June 20, 1779, and by August, two thousand head of Texas cattle, gathered from the ranches of the missions and individuals in the Béxar-La Bahía region, were on their way to Gálvez's forces in Louisiana.

During the remainder of the American Revolution—1779, 1780, 1781, and 1782—over nine thousand head of Texas cattle, known for sure, were rounded up on the ranches between Béxar and La Bahía and were trailed overland into Louisiana. From La Bahía, the assembly point, herds were trailed to Nacogdoches, Natchitoches, and Opelousas for distribution to Spanish forces.

Spanish Texas cattlemen and their *vaqueros* trailed these cattle. Soldiers from Béxar, La Bahía, and El Fuerte del Cíbolo escorted the herds. Several hundred head of horses were also sent along for cavalry and artillery purposes. Extant records even indicate that a few soldiers from Texas were recruited to fight with Gálvez's army.

And the upshot of the story is this: Fueled in part by Texas beef—Texas Longhorns, nonetheless—Spanish troops took to the field in the fall of 1779 and defeated the British in battles at Manchac, Baton Rouge, and Natchez. (This sounds like the Civil War, but it isn't—it's the American Revolution!)

The next spring, after a month-long siege by land and sea

46

forces, Gálvez, with over 2000 men, captured the British stronghold at Mobile on March 14, 1780.

The climax to the Gulf Coast campaign occurred the following year when Gálvez directed a two-pronged land and sea attack on Pensacola, the British capital of West Florida. Over 7000 men were involved in the two-month-long siege of Pensacola before its capture on May 10, 1781.

Although Lord Cornwallis surrendered to George Washington at Yorktown on October 19, 1781, the war was not over for the Spaniards. Gálvez organized an expedition, which on May 8, 1782, captured the British naval base at New Providence in the Bahamas. And he was busy preparing his greatest campaign yet against the British in Jamaica when peace negotiations ended the war in 1783.

By defeating the British along the entire Gulf Coast, Gálvez and his Spanish forces made it a whole lot easier for George Washington and his Continental Army to fight and defeat the British along the eastern seaboard.

As we continue to commemorate the American Revolution, therefore, let us give due credit to Gálvez and his Spanish troops. And let us not forget the interesting and uniquely significant role that Texas—and the Texas Longhorns—played in the winning of American independence.

Now for the historical facts to verify and corroborate this story—

Early in 1778, the first commandant-general of the interior provinces of New Spain, Teodoro de Croix, visited Texas on an inspection tour of his new command. He took special notice of the many ranches and the great herds of cattle between Béxar and La Bahía. Recognizing the ranching industry as a source of royal revenue, he issued sweeping new regulations for the Texas cattle industry. All unappropriated lands not granted to the missions or individuals, he decreed, belonged to the Royal Hacienda, and thenceforth all strayed and unbranded animals were the property of the crown. Citizens who gathered and branded unmarked animals were required to obtain a license and pay a tax of four *reales* (one *peso* was worth eight *reales,* or "eight bits'') per head for cattle and six *reales* for horses.[1]

Croix allowed a grace period of four months for the ranchers to round up and brand their stock and to register their brands.[2] Thereafter, all unbranded, wild, or strayed animals would be subject to the tax. The governor was ordered to keep a record of all brands, fees, and animals exported from the province. Unaccustomed to such regulation, both the missionaries and the private ranchers greeted the decree with a storm of protest but with little effect.[3] The Croix decree, however, did set the stage for the legal exportation of cattle in 1779.

It appears that small herds of cattle had been driven to supply presidial troops in Coahuila and Nuevo Santander before the decree, but the legal exportation of cattle from the Province of Texas did not open until June, 1779. Francisco García, an emissary of Governor Bernardo de Gálvez, arrived in San Antonio de Bexar on June 20th with a letter to Texas Governor Domingo Cabello requesting the delivery of two thousand head of cattle from Texas to Louisiana. At this time, Gálvez had not received official word of Spain's declaration of war yet, but he anticipated war and began to prepare for it. Following orders that forbade trade with Louisiana, Cabello refused until the commandant-general's wishes were ascertained. Croix replied on August 16, 1779, as follows:

> All that your Lordship has done—which you report in your *oficio* number 72 of June 20th last—has struck me well. You report that, until you know my decision, you will not permit the removal of fifteen hundred or two thousand head of cattle requested by the *señor* governor of La Luisiana, *don*

1. Weddle and Thonhoff, *Drama & Conflict: The Texas Saga of 1776,* 169; Faulk, *The Last Years of Spanish Texas, 1778-1821,* 85; Sandra L. Myres, *The Ranch in Spanish Texas, 1691-1800* (Social Science Series Number 2, The University of Texas at El Paso, 1969), 37.

2. Faulk, *The Last Years of Spanish Texas,* 1778-1821, 85.

3. *Ibid.;* Myres, *The Ranch in Spanish Texas, 1691-1800,* 37-38.

Bernardo de Gálvez, who has sent his representative Francisco García to gather them up. But because dispatching this livestock to the aforementioned governor is expedient to the service of the king, I dispose that Your Lordship proceed immediately to its purchase and roundup, taking care that the number of beasts includes sufficient bulls so that the stock may procreate in that region [La Luisiana] and so that the breed does not become scarce or extinct in the province under Your Lordship's command.

In this regard Your Lordship is to avail yourself of the assistance of the president of the missions, *fray* Pedro Ramíres, disposing that the stock be rounded up from among the missions and residents. Your Lordship is to arrange the necessary escort service, the escort to be composed of residents and troops, according as the prompt delivery of the stock may thereby be facilitated. And your Lordship is to render with preference over all [other requests], whatever services the aforementioned governor might request of you, advising me later of the nature of his requests and whether they have been granted.[4]

Croix went on to grant Governor Cabello broad, sweeping authority to permit the exportation of livestock as he saw fit, even to the extent of imposing a "moderate duty on each head of stock taken out, in order to defray the costs of the military."[5]

In another communication dated September 20, 1779, Cabello wrote Croix that measures for carrying out the exportation of two thousand head of cattle, including a number of bulls, under consignment to the governor of Louisiana were being taken. Cabello had conferred with Fray Pedro Ramíres de

4. Croix to Cabello, August 16, 1779, Bexar Archives. Researchers will be glad to know that there are Bexar Archives Translations (BAT), an on-going project, up to the year 1787. Hereafter, for their convenience, the BAT file number, volume, and page numbers will be given in parentheses, as in this instance, (BAT 2C342, vol. 85, pp. 112-114).

5. *Ibid.*

Arellano, *presidente* of Texas missions, to whom Gálvez had sent his request and contract. Fray Ramíres agreed to the request and contract, but a few difficulties had arisen. For one thing, Francisco García, who was to take charge of the herd, had already returned to New Orleans. Another was that most of the cattle belonging to the mission of Espíritu Santo, from whom the major part of the herd came, was unbranded stock, which presented legal questions. Furthermore, because many of the cattle were from pasturelands under dispute between Cíbolo ranchers and the Espíritu Santo mission, Cabello decided that the cattle from the mission would be gathered only between Presidio La Bahía and the coast. Additional cattle were obtained from Mission Rosario and area ranchers to fill out the herd. In the event that Francisco García could not be located, the herd would be delivered to Opelousas, where Gálvez was asked to arrange for someone to receive them.[6]

Archival records regarding the details of these first cattle drives are fragmentary, scattered, and sketchy. When pieced together, like a jigsaw puzzle with many parts missing, the composite picture has many skips and gaps in it, hopefully which later research will resolve.

One of the most puzzling of the cattle drives regards a delivery that was made in August, 1779. But one has to glean through all the Bexar Archives records through 1786 to pick out pieces to the story.

Acting as agents to secure cattle from Texas were two prominent traders, Nicolás de la Mathe and Francisco Rosé, who had business connections in New Orleans, Opelousas, Natchitoches, Nacogdoches, La Bahía, and Béxar. These two men acted in liaison with political, military, and religious authorities in Louisiana and Texas to effect the delivery of cattle requested by Gálvez.

Sometime during the summer of 1779, Nicolás de la Mathe secured a passport for the delivery of nine hundred head of cattle. Juan de Ysurieta, a Béxar businessman, acted as his agent to

6. *Ibid.*

buy a herd. Most of the cattle were assembled at the Rancho de San Francisco and placed under the supervision of Joseph Félix Menchaca, senior lieutenant at the Presidio San Antonio de Béxar and operator of the Rancho de San Francisco. (Menchaca also resided in the commandancy of the presidio, later known as the Spanish Governor's Palace—Governor Cabello resided in the *Casas Reales,* or Royal Buildings, on the east side of Main Plaza.) Included in the herd were 180 cattle that belonged to the Mission San Antonio de Valero, probably from its nearby Rancho de la Mora. Mixed in with the herd were 40 bulls belonging to Juan Joseph Pacheco. Another 30 head were taken along to cover losses along the way, bringing the herd total to 970 head.[7]

Because the direct road going from Béxar to Nacogdoches had been cut off by Comanches for a number of years, the herd was conducted along a southeast detour from Béxar, taking it past El Fuerte del Cíbolo and then eastward to join the La Bahía-Nacogdoches Road. Crossing the Trinity River near old Bucareli, the herd was trailed to Nacogdoches, where it was inspected by Captain Antonio Gil Ybarbo on August 30, 1779. Finding the herd in excess of its passport, Ybarbo, alleged Menchaca in later court proceedings, confiscated thirty-seven bulls belonging to Pacheco, that did not have a license. The remainder were allowed to go to Opelousas, where Menchaca sold them to Monsieur Bodore for 11 *pesos* each. In long, drawn-out court proceedings, under litigation till 1786, Pacheco sued Menchaca for the value of the thirty-seven bulls, which he claimed Menchaca sold with the rest in Opelousas. Interesting as the court records are, the main point for the story here is the fact that 970 head of cattle were trailed from Texas to Louisiana in August, 1779, by Joseph Félix Menchaca, Juan de Ysurieta, Juan Joseph Pacheco, Francisco Pérez, Albert Giménez (Ximénez), and other "boys" who were driving the herd.[8]

7. *Auto,* Domingo Cabello, April 30, 1784, Bexar Archives (BAT, 2C40, vol. 97, 63-66).

8. Proceedings, June 2, 1780-July 5, 1780, Bexar Archives (BAT, 2C40, vol. 97, 31-37).

Related to this drive, which appears to be the first one in response to Gálvez's request, is an inclusion in a letter dated August 30, 1779, from Louis Jean Césaire Bormé, Commandant at Natchitoches, to Gálvez. Bormé wrote:

> My Governor: I received on the 25th, by M. Rosé, who left Opelusas the 22d of the same month, the dispatches which you addressed to M. De Mézières, Don Antonio Gil Y Barbo, Juachín Hortega, and Francisco García, who has read your letter, having just arrived at that moment and being obliged to depart tomorrow for town.
>
> There have arrived at this post from St. Antoine [San Antonio], Don Juan Bautista y Surrieta [Ysurieta], Don Miguel Minchaca [Menchaca, nephew to Joseph Félix Menchaca], and Pacheco [probably Juan Joseph Pacheco], who are hastening to go to the capital to see your Excellency. They are taking some horses, of which they will tell you the number, as well as their intentions regarding them.[9]

It appears from the two foregoing instances that while Joseph Félix Menchaca was with the main herd in Nacogdoches on August 30th, these three other men had gone on ahead with a herd of horses to make necessary arrangements for the delivery of the cattle. Ysurieta, Miguel Menchaca, and Pacheco were in Natchitoches the same day Joseph Félix Menchaca was in Nacogdoches. The former three, according to Bormé's letter, were on their way to see Governor Gálvez in New Orleans.

Another clue regarding the delivery of this first herd is found in a letter from Cabello to Croix, dated October 19, 1779. Concerned about his troop strength, Cabello wrote:

> Of 82 privates *de cuera* and *ligero* which this company has, 19 are detached to El Cíbolo, 3 are in

9. Herbert Eugene Botlon (Ed.), *Athanase de Mézières and the Louisiana-Texas Frontier, 1769-1780* (2 vols., Cleveland, 1914), II, 266-267.

the abilitado's party, 6 are with the party in Coahuila in search of tobacco for the *estanco*, 22 are in the horseherd, 21 have gone with Lieutenant Menchaca, and 1 is sick, with the result that 10 men are left free for service.

What has worried me most is having to take away from their training the 30 recruits whom I have had to send to serve in the detachments at the fort and with the horseherd, and taking away from those duties soldiers who are prepared for the journey upon which I have sent Lieutenant Joseph Menchaca because of its importance—as I disclose to your Lordship in the *ofisio* pertaining to this matter.[10]

A few words need to be said about Joseph Félix Menchaca, a key figure in the first cattle deliveries. The Menchaca family was one of the most prominent families of San Antonio. They descended from Francisco Menchaca, who had come there with the founding expedition of Martin de Alarcón. The eldest son, Luís Antonio, enhanced his postion by marrying the daughter of José de Urrútia, captain of the presidio from 1733 to 1740. Urrútia himself had married the daughter of Captain Diego Ramón, one-time lieutenant of Alonso de León who led the search-for-La Salle expedition into Texas in 1690. Luís Antonio succeeded his brother-in-law, Toribio de Urrútia, as captain of the Presidio San Antonio de Béxar in 1763. Upon his retirement, Luís Antonio's brother, Joseph Félix Menchaca, became the senior ranking officer at the presidio under the governor, who was captain. Joseph Félix Menchaca, in addition to residing in the *commandancia* of the presidio (now called the Spanish Governor's Palace), was the co-operator with his brother, Luís Antonio, of the Rancho de San Francisco, named in honor of their father.[11] Typifying the classical Texas example of the

10. Cabello to Croix, October 19, 1779, Bexar Archives (BAT, 2C36, vol. 88, 60-66).
11. Weddle and Thonhoff, *Drama & Conflict: The Texas Saga of 1776*, 61-62; 145-146.

criollo vs. peninsular feelings of the time, the Menchacas were at odds often with both Governor Cabello and his predecessor, Barón de Ripperdá.

On August 17, 1779, Croix sent Cabello a letter regarding the exportation of three hundred head of cattle from Béxar to Natchitoches. Doña María de St. Denís, a resident of the Presidio of Natchitoches, had acquired them in Béxar, and Croix advised Cabello to grant her request that her agent (and relative), Don Félix Menchaca, be allowed to drive her cattle to her.[12] On September 15th, Cabello notified Croix that he acceded to her request.[13] Conceivably, these cattle could have been taken along with the others by Menchaca on his first drive, or they could have been taken in a subsequent drive in the fall. The records do not indicate what finally happened.

Although Spain declared war against Great Britain on May 8, 1779, Gálvez did not receive official word of it in New Orleans till the following August. Official notification did not reach Teodoro de Croix in Chihuahua until October, whereupon he dispatched a letter on October 7th to Governor Cabello with an attached bando quoting His Catholic Majesty's declaration of war against the king, realms, and subjects of Great Britain, which is noted in part as follows:

> Whereas the Most Excellent Senor Don Josef de Gálvez, by royal order of last May 8, advises me of the following:
> "The king. . .has decided to declare war on [the king] of Great Britain, and [has decreed] that upon receipt of this order, it is to be published by solemn bando throughout America". . . .I command the [provincial] governors quickly to have copies of the *bando* made, published, and placed in the most public locations in the towns, villas, and [other] places under

12. Croix to Cabello, August 17, 1779, Bexar Archives (BAT, 2C342, vol. 86, 1).

13. Cabello to Croix, September 15, 1779, Bexar Archives (BAT, 2C343, vol. 87, 38-39).

[the jurisdiction of] their respective governments, that it may come to the attention of all.[14]

It took two more months for the news to reach Governor Cabello in Texas. In a certified act of obedience, Cabello tells of the receipt and disposition of the royal resolution:

> In the Royal Presidio of San Antonio de Béxar on the tenth day of the month of December in the year seventeen hundred seventy-nine, I, *don* Domingo Cabello, colonel of the royal armies, governor and commander of the armies of the province of Los Texas, its missions, conquests and frontiers, captain of the cavalry company of the royal presidio of San Antonio de Béxar, inspector general of the corps of militia and presidial troops of the said province by commission conferred by the lord commandant general of the Interior Provinces of this kingdom of New Spain, say that, having received in the mail which arrived at this presidio yesterday...the royal order in which His Majesty (God save him) has decided to declare war on the king of Great Britain...And so that all citizens, residents, and dwellers included in the district under my command may be aware of this royal resolution, it is to be published as a *bando* in the usual streets and plazas to the sound of drums; and so that the same procedure may take place in the royal presidio of La Bahía del Espíritu Santo and in the town of Nuestra Señora del Pilár de Nacogdoches, the only remaining places under this government, let two notarized copies be made and sent to the commander and the lieutenant governor of those settlements, respectively, who, after having [the *bandos*] published as mentioned, are to place them in their respective archives...[15]

14. Croix to Cabello, October 7, 1779, Bexar Archives (BAT, 2C36, vol. 88, 22-25).

15. Act of Obedience, December 10, 1779, Bexar Archives (BAT, 2C36, vol. 88, 25-27).

On December 13, 1779, the populace of the Villa de San Fernando de Béxar learned of the declaration of war, shown by the following attachment to the foregoing Act of Obedience:

> Béxar, December 13, 1779
> On this date the bando was published as ordered in the preceding act, and copies were sent to the presidio of La Bahía and to the town of Nacogdoches; and for your knowledge I make haste thus to certify.
>
> Cabello[16]
> [Rubric]

Presumably, the *bando* was forwarded to chief officers at La Bahía and Nacogdoches in the next dispatch of mail, which had been established on a monthly basis by Croix earlier that year.[17] In charge of the Presidio La Bahía at this time was Captain Luis Cazorla. The Lieutenant Governor of the Villa de Nacogdoches was Antonio Gil Ybarbo.

The presidios at San Antonio and La Bahía were required to submit a monthly roster listing the names of men, stating presence or absence, and noting the assignment for each on the date of the roster. Only a few muster rolls for the years of this study are extant in the Bexar Archives. (Perhaps others can be found in the Archives of the Indies in Guadalajara or Seville.) The muster roll for the company of cavalry at Presidio La Bahía for the date December 1, 1779 (see Appendix), provides a clue to cattle driving activities then. Listed as "CP. [Counted Present] on Detached Duty" are the names of privates Josef Contreras, Juan Josef Martinez, Francisco Antonio Buentello, and Pedro Josef Grande. On the summary sheet, four men were listed as "Ydem [Privates] as escorts or on detached duty."[18] It is possible that these men were escorting a herd of cattle from La Bahía to Gálvez's forces in Louisiana.

16. *Ibid.*, December 13, 1779.
17. Weddle and Thonhoff, *Drama & Conflict: The Texas Saga of 1776*, 69.
18. Cavalry Company of the Royal Presidio of La Bahía del Espíritu Santo, December 1, 1779, Bexar Archives (BAT, 2C37, vol. 90, 44-48).

A confidential letter from Cabello to Croix dated December 20, 1779, describes activities in Texas during the remainder of the year. Cabello, who was suffering from a dislocated left shoulder, planned a trip to Presidio La Bahía on December 24th to review and reorganize the cavalry company there. While absent from the Presidio de Béxar, he placed 1st Lieutenant Joseph Félix Menchaca in command there. To care for political matters, he named as interim lieutenant governor Joseph Antonio Curbelo. On his journey to La Bahía, Cabello wanted to examine the fort at El Cíbolo, for he believed it to be improperly located by his predecessor, Barón de Ripperdá. And, finally, he mentioned that when Francisco García returned to the *villa* of New Orleans, García asked the governor to provide him with a man to serve as a guide and two others to care for his pack mules and horses. Cabello put Ygnacio Peña, "a citizen of this *villa* and *presidio*," in charge of the assignment with two other boys, who accompanied García as far as "El Apelusan" (Opelousas).[19]

Another document bearing the same date of December 20, 1779, makes bare mention of a herd of cattle exported by the Mission Rosario. Without mentioning purpose, destination, number, or other details, the notation in an inventory of papers for 1778-1779 reads as follows:

> No. 51 Copy of proceedings concerning the exportation of a herd of *orejana* [unbranded] cattle from the mission of El Rosario at La Bahía del Espíritu Santo.[20]

No other record for this herd could be found in the Bexar Archives. It could be speculated, perhaps, that there might be a connection between this herd and the four soldiers from La Bahía who were listed as "escorts on detached duty" on December 1, 1779.

19. Cabello to Croix, December 20, 1779, Bexar Archives (BAT, 2C37, vol. 90, 85-88).
20. Inventory of Papers, 1778-1779, December 20, 1779, Bexar Archives (BAT, 2C37, vol. 90, 83).

Thus ended the year 1779.

The need for additional food supplies, especially cattle from Texas, by Gálvez, as he prepared for his Mobile campaign in the winter of 1779-1780, must have been serious. The previous August 24th, it will be remembered, a hurricane struck lower Louisiana just as he was preparing for his march against Fort Bute at Manchac. Inundation was extreme in the Attakapas-Opelousas area. The Mississippi rose to the greatest height within memory of the oldest inhabitants. Cattle in the region were decimated.[21] The need for more beef was urgent, and it appears that more Texas cattle were trailed to Louisiana that winter and following spring, but documentary details are very sketchy.

Meantime, war and preparation for war continued. Back at Presidio La Bahía, Governor Cabello received another communication from Commandant-General Croix, this time conveying the wishes of His Catholic Majesty King Carlos III upon his subjects in Texas. The royal order read as follows:

> The King, moved by his mercy and desire to implore before all things the protection of the Almighty, upon whom the destinies of empires and the fate of wars depend, has commanded that in all his dominions of Spain and America public rogations be offered for the success and felicity of his Catholic armed forces. I am informing you of his wishes by royal order, that you may immediately put into effect this pious obligation in all the towns under your command.[22]

The royal order for prayers in America for success in war was received by Governor Cabello, who, on April 20, 1780, complied as follows:

21. Martin, *The History of Louisiana,* 235.
22. Croix to Cabello, February 18, 1780, Bexar Archives (BAT, 2C39, vol. 93, 72).

I have sent my official letter enclosing the above order to the most reverend *padre presidente* of the missions of this province, the *padre cura* of the *villa* of San Fernando, and the chaplain of this *presidio,* that they may proceed with that which his Majesty commands and which the lord commandant-general orders. Let this original be kept in the archives of this provincial government as evidence that this royal decision has been observed.[23]

Still recovering at La Bahia from his dislocated arm, to which was applied "fomentations of lion fat" as a poultice, Governor Cabello, on March 18th, wrote El Cavallero de Croix that he had not heard lately from Governor Gálvez regarding the cattle that Gálvez had ordered. Cabello wrote:

The lieutenant at the post of Natchitoches has written me the enclosed letter, which although it may serve to burden your Lordship, I send it to you in order that you may be advised of its contents—even though you may already have received the same news from the *cavallero* governor of La Luiciana. That governor has me concerned, for he has not answered the letters I have written him about the subject of cattle.[24]

The reason, of course, that Cabello had not heard from Gálvez was that Gálvez was in the midst of his campaign against Fort Charlotte at Mobile, which capitulated on March 14th—in partial answer to the prayers of the Spanish faithful everywhere.

A clue to the delivery of cattle to Gálvez's forces in the spring of 1780 is found in a bit of trouble that cropped up be-

---

23. Cabello to Croix, April 20, 1780, Bexar Archives (BAT, 2C39, vol. 93, 73).

24. Cabello to Croix, March 18, 1780, Bexar Archives (BAT, 2C39, vol. 94, 68-69).

tween Governor Cabello and Francisco Flores, Joseph Félix Menchaca, Juan de Ysurieta, and a few others. It concerned the confiscation of two wicker baskets containing bundles of tobacco and two trunks containing fabrics from Louisiana. According to fragmentary records, Cabello, who was still at La Bahía, was informed by the guard that at 8:30 P.M., April 25, 1780, Francisco Flores, his servant Julian de Orosco, and Lorenzo Reñe, had just arrived at the gate of the presidio. They had just come from Louisiana. Suspicious of their appearance and actions, Cabello queried the two servant boys and learned that Flores, Joseph Félix Menchaca, Juan de Ysurieta, Agustín Ruíz, and Félix Guerrero had just returned from a trip to Louisiana. From Opelousas, where they delivered a herd of cattle, they took a side trip to New Orleans and went on a little shopping spree. Stern questioning made the two boys confess that they had hidden that afternoon, in a large ditch a half league from the presidio, two leather trunks containing Brittany, Rouen, and West Indian cloth and some other trifles that Flores had bought in New Orleans. Also hidden in the same place were two wicker baskets containing bundles of tobacco, bought in Opelousas by Ruíz and Guerrero. Further, Don Félix Menchaca and Don Juan de Ysurieta had traveled with the group from Opelousas, but left them at the Colorado River to go directly to the Rancho de San Francisco. The rest of the group went to La Bahía. Menchaca and Ysurieta (married to a niece of the Menchacas) were themselves carrying about five loads of clothing, as well as other effects, plus a young negress slave whom Ysurieta had purchased in New Orleans.[25]

In order to substantiate that the tobacco was contraband and that the other goods were brought in without license or payment of taxes, Cabello took statements from the informants and ordered soldiers, accompanied by the two boys, to proceed to the ditch and confiscate the goods. A few days later, at Béxar, Menchaca and Ysurieta turned themselves in and surrendered

25. Cabello to Croix, May 9, 1780, Bexar Archives (BAT, 2C40, vol. 96, 14-20); *Auto,* Domingo Cabello, October 26, 1782, Bexar Archives (BAT, 2C47, vol. 113, 69-74).

several loads of goods. After much searching, soldiers from Béxar found the rest of the goods hidden not far from San Antonio, whereupon Flores, Menchaca, and Ysurieta were chastized by the governor for introducing contraband goods without the required payment of tax. The worst that the governor could prove on Menchaca, his arch-adversary, was that he used some of the blue cloth to make a new uniform.[26]

News of Gálvez's success at Mobile was not long in reaching Cabello, who relayed it to Croix, as is shown by this letter dated June 2, 1780, from Croix to Cabello:

> I am grateful for the news from Louisiana which your Lordship has seen fit to communicate to me. That of the taking of Mobile by Colonel Bernardo de Gálvez has been confirmed by courier who went from New Orleans to Vera Cruz with additional news that that same commander [Gálvez] was to order an expedition by land against Pensacola, and another going by sea under the command of *don* Juan Bautista Bonet.[27]

After the capture of Mobile on March 14, 1780, Gálvez started preparing for a campaign against Pensacola that fall. Mobile would be used as a supply base, stocked with cattle as well as other military supplies, as this letter from Diego Joseph Navarro, Captain-General of Cuba, written to Viceroy Martín de Mayorga on February 7, 1780, indicates:

> The adverse weather which has been prevailing has not permitted the departure of the convoy and transports of the 1,412 for Mobile. The governor of Louisiana was advised of these preparations and informed that, after the departure of these troops, more would be prepared if he requested them in

26. *Ibid.*
27. Croix to Cabello, June 2, 1780, Bexar Archives (BAT, 2C40, vol. 97, 16-17).

order to continue the conquest of Pensacola.

At the same time as the departure of this vessel [carrying the letter to Mayorga], the warships are sailing for Mobile and Louisiana to support that governor in case he has begun his siege . . .

The said governor [Gálvez] had received . . . the letter [which] advised him what had been done at this post [Havana] for the prompt dispatch of 1,200 troops and 200 laborers for artillery and fortification work, together with the corresponding equipment, munitions, and provisions, so that, together with the forces assembled in that province [Louisiana], he might undertake the conquest of Mobile. The letter stated that, after the departure of this convoy, the work of preparing troops, train, etc., intended for the enterprise against Pensacola would be continued, so that they could be dispatched when requested by *Don* Bernardo de Gálvez from Mobile. Consequently the latter [Gálvez] decided to send Miró to explain that it was desirable that the said increase of forces, train, and munitions should be dispatched immediately in as large numbers as possible, with provisions for four months, and supplies of salt to make salt meat from the cattle found in Mobile, and that subsequently a vessel should be sent every fifteen days or every month with provisions for the replenishment of those consumed by the expedition.[28]

Spanish correspondence for this time indicates that the food staples for an army on the move included *carne salada* (salt meat), *carne fresca* (fresh meat), *harinas* (flour), and *menestras* (vegetables for soup).[29] The foregoing letter specifically asks for

28. Navarro to Mayorga, February 7, 1780, as cited in Kinnaird, *Spain in the Mississippi Valley, 1765-1794*, II, 368-373.

29. Mayorga to Joseph de Gálvez, July 31, 1781, Archivo General de las Indias, Audiencia de Santo Domingo (University of Texas at Austin Archives, AGI, vol. 142, 406-407).

salt to make salt meat, undoubtedly from cattle that were delivered to the army from Louisiana.

On May 30, 1780, Marcos Hernández, a resident of La Bahía applied for a passport to transport 1500 head of cattle that he purchased from Mission Espíritu Santo to the "pueblo of La Apeluza" in the province of Louisiana. Governor Cabello granted the permit, but on condition that Hernández pay a duty of two *reales* for each head of cattle that he exported. Hernández gathered the cattle at the Arroyo de los Nogales, one of the pasture grounds belonging to Espíritu Santo. *Don* Phelipe Flores, a resident of Béxar, was commissioned to oversee the roundup and the count. Upon the payment of three hundred eight *pesos* and four *reales,* Hernández was permitted to trail a herd of 1234 Texas Longhorns to Gálvez's forces in Louisiana.[30] By this time Gálvez had taken Mobile, and Pensacola was his next target.

Disastrous misfortune befell the next shipment of Texas cattle to Gálvez. Comanche Indians had become bolder than ever, and from their hill country hideaways they descended the Cíbolo and Guadalupe river valleys to depredate the ranchos between Béxar and La Bahía, killing and stealing cattle and horses by the wholesale. Ensconced on a ridge between the Guadalupe and Colorado rivers, dubbed El Monte del Diablo by the Spaniards,[31] the Comanches waylaid traffic on the road between La Bahía and Nacogdoches, over which the Texas cattle were also trailed.

First indication of this is given in a letter from Cabello to Croix, written at La Bahía on July 10, 1780. In it Cabello expressed great concern at not having received a reply from the *cavallero* governor of La Luciana regarding the export of one or two thousand head of cattle that were requested, undoubtedly for the Pensacola campaign planned that fall. Cabello, however, had received a letter on June 21st from Jose Foucher, secretary of

30. Cabello to Croix, May 30, 1780; June 1, 1780; June 23, 1780; October 12, 1780; October 13, 1780; Bexar Archives (BAT, 2C40, vol. 96, 49-62).

31. Elizabeth A.H. John, *Storms Brewed in Other Men's Worlds* (College Station, Texas, 1975), 617.

Governor Gálvez, specifying the number to be two thousand.[32]

At the same time, Cabello had received another letter from Fray Pedro Ramírez, the reverend *padre presidente* of the Texas missions, who informed Cabello that Fray José María de Escobar, *ministro* of Mission Espíritu Santo, would provide as many head as could be rounded up for export to Gálvez. In addition, Don Cristóbal Ylario de Córdoba had recently come from San Antonio de Béxar with twenty men whom he had hired by authority of the *padre presidente*. Córdoba informed the governor that he had come to take charge of driving the herd as far as Nacogdoches, "where it would be possible to drive it wherever the *cavallero* Don Bernardo de Gálvez might direct."[33]

Córdoba added that Gálvez and the *padre presidente* had decided between them that the entire two thousand head should not be exported at one time, but that there should be two drives of one thousand head each. Córdoba, after delivering the first herd, would return to La Bahía for the second. Thirteen hundred head of cattle were rounded up on the pastures of Espíritu Santo, and armed with the necessary passports and letters for Ybarbo and Foucher, Córdoba and his men set out for Nacogdoches with the first herd. Awaiting the return of Córdoba to La Bahía, Cabello received a letter on July 3rd informing him that disaster befell Córdoba and all the men driving the herd. They were attacked by Comanche Indians, who had now appeared and were "making continuous invasions into this unfortunate province from the direction of the Guadalupe River."[34]

With this latest calamity both the roundup and exportation were curtailed for now, moaned Cabello, "the latter because the chief person who knows how to guide the herd has gone to Nacogdoches; the former, because all the people in this province are so intimidated that I would not be able to find anyone who for any amount of money whatever would expose

32. Cabello to Croix, July 10, 1780, Bexar Archives (BAT, 2C41, vol. 100, 16-20).
33. *Ibid.*
34. *Ibid.*

himself to the dangers that these people are facing." Even the padres were reluctant to expose their cattle to the imminent danger posed by the Comanches.[35]

Few if any cattle on this shipment evidently reached Nacogdoches, and there is no record of a second shipment. The only thing known for certain is that Córdoba himself reached Nacogdoches and that he wrote Cabello a letter telling of his misfortune.

Comanche troubles dominated the correspondence of Cabello the rest of the summer. He wrote that on the night of June 18th, hostile Indians drove off part of the horse herds at the ranches of San Bartólo and Las Mulas, both close to El Fuerte del Cíbolo. A corporal and nine privates pursued the hostiles to the Guadalupe River. Don Tomás Travieso, owner of Las Mulas, went with them. Finding such a great multitude of Indians on the opposite bank of the river, the force returned to El Cíbolo and sent word for reinforcements from Bexar. *Alférez* don Marcelo Váldez set out, accompanied by one sergeant, four corporals, thirty-seven soldiers, four citizens, and ten Indians from the missions at Béxar. Numbering sixty-seven, the force found that the Comanche horde had increased in number, and they called for more reinforcements. Lt. Joseph Félix Menchaca left Béxar with ten more soldiers, six citizens, and fourteen Indians. They were joined by one sergeant, two corporals, and nine privates sent out from Presidio La Bahía. This combined force of 110 men followed the Comanches to a place called Gerónimo Flores' water spring, where they judiciously decided to call of an attack because they were still so greatly outnumbered by enemy Indians.[36]

On July 3rd, Cabello received news at La Bahía that hostiles numbering about a hundred had made an attack at a place called the Arroyo de Los Nogales, where a herd of cattle was being rounded up for exportation to the *cavallero* governor of La Luiciana. The attack resulted in the death of one man and in the

35. *Ibid.*
36. Cabello to Croix, July 17, 1780, Bexar Archives (BAT, 2C41, vol. 100, 37-49).

wounding of two others making the roundup.[37]

The night of July 11, 1780, Cabello received a message from the alférez detached to El Fuerte del Cíbolo. A group of Comanche Indians had arrived at the Rancho de San Bartólo that morning. After killing two herdsmen, they drove off all the cows and calves, and they also broke down the door of the house and destroyed all the furniture inside.[38] This prompted Cabello to lament that:

> Not a moment passes in which news of rapacities and catastrophies does not reach me. All these ranchos find themselves completely helpless and abandoned. And from this will result the total destruction and loss of this province.[39]

Still at La Bahía, Cabello wrote a letter on August 10th that contained a record of events that occurred since his last communication with Croix. One vacancy existed in the company at Presidio San Antonio de Béxar with the killing of one *de cuera* soldier by Comanche Indians. He asked Croix to consider how it was possible, with such a small number of men left after providing for the great number of duties these troops had to discharge (including, undoubtedly, escort service for cattle drives), for the remaining troops to be able to quell the incessant armed aggression he faced—not only in the region of Bexar, but also in the region of La Bahía. He had dispatched two sergeants and six men to go to the *villas* along the Río Grande in the colony of Nuevo Santander to buy seventy or eighty horses and some mules to replace mounts stolen by the Comanches. In view of the hopeless situation he faced, Cabello regretted that he could not reinforce El Fuerte del Cíbolo with another twenty or thirty men to protect the adjacent ranchos from further assault by hostile Indians.[40]

37. *Ibid.*
38. *Ibid.*
39. *Ibid.*
40. Cabello to Croix, August 10, 1780, Bexar Archives (BAT, 2C41, vol. 100, 73-76).

Mission San Antonio de Valero, popularly known as the Alamo, owned and operated the Rancho de la Mora near present Falls City, Texas.

(Photo courtesy of Institute of Texan Cultures)

Mission Concepción owned and operated the Rancho del Paistle near present Lavernia, Texas.

Mission San José de Aguayo owned and operated the Rancho del Atascoso in the present Pleasanton-Poteet-Lytle, Texas, area.

(Photo courtesy of Institute of Texan Cultures)

Mission San Juan Capistrano owned and operated the Rancho de Pataguilla near present Panna Maria and Hobson, Texas.

(Photo courtesy of Institute of Texan Cultures)

Mission San Francisco de la Espada owned and operated the Rancho de las Cabras near present Floresville, Texas.

(Photo courtesy of Institute of Texan Cultures)

Spanish Governor's Palace, formerly the *comandancia* of the Presidio de San Antonio de Béxar, which provided troop escorts for trail drives to Louisiana, 1779-1782.

(Photo courtesy of Institute of Texan Cultures)

Mission Espíritu Santo, which supplied most of the Texas Longhorn cattle for Spanish Forces during the American Revolution.

(Photo courtesy of Institute of Texan Cultures)

Ruins of Mission Rosario, which supplied some of the cattle trailed to Louisiana, 1779-1782.

(Photo courtesy of James H. Sutton, Jr., of San Antonio, Texas)

Presidio La Bahía, which supplied some of the troop escorts for the Texas Longhorn cattle delivered to Bernardo de Gálvez's forces.

(Photo courtesy of James H. Sutton, Jr., of San Antonio, Texas)

Photo of Carvajal Dugout, ancient structure, now gone, on Rancho de San Bartólo, the first private ranch in Texas, near present Czestochowa, Texas.

(Photo courtesy of Mrs. Helmuth H. Schuenemann of Kenedy, Texas)

Photo of old stone tomb, now gone, which was near El Fuerte del Cibolo in present Karnes County, Texas.
(Photo courtesy of Mrs. Helmuth H. Schuenemann of Kenedy, Texas)

Old Stone Fort at Nacogdoches, where Texas Longhorns were trailed on way to Opelousas.

(Photo courtesy of Institute of Texan Cultures)

Artist's conception of Spanish *rancheros* in the eighteenth century.

(Photo courtesy of Institute of Texan Cultures)

M. Emanuel

Artist's conception of Capt. Bernardo D'Ortolant, *circa* 1780, leading troopers of military cavalry through East Texas.

(Photo courtesy of Institute of Texan Cultures)

Governor Cabello, after a nine-month stay at La Bahía, returned to his headquarters at Béxar in September. On his way, he stopped to inspect El Fuerte del Cíbolo. He was astonished that his predecessor, Barón de Ripperdá, had situated the fort "in the most inappropriate, strange, and unusual site that could be chosen." Based on his previous military experience in Nicaragua, Cabello proposed to relocate the fort "at a more appropriate, suitable, and fitting site," whereby it could provide protection not only to the ranchos on the banks of Cibolo Creek but also to those along the San Antonio River.[41]

Compounding Cabello's troubles at this time was the problem of command at both his presidios. Don Luís Cazorla would soon be retiring, and Cabello thought that Lieutenant José Santoja was totally unfit for command. Nor could either of the two lieutenants at Béxar replace Cazorla. Second Lieutenant Bernardo de Fernández had just been commissioned by Croix to go to the pueblo of El Paso del Norte as deputy governor. The first lieutenant at Béxar, Joseph Félix Menchaca, could not be recommended by Cabello because "his bad conduct makes him unworthy of consideration of anything." Because of the longstanding feud between the Menchacas and the governor, Cabello recommended the transfer of Joseph Félix to the Presidio San Juan Bautista del Río Grande, which was effected by the end of the year.[42]

Hardly had a week passed since Cabello's visit to El Fuerte del Cíbolo, when seventy Comanches, suddenly springing from a large gully north of the fort, attacked it. One soldier, Julian Rondeín, who was an interpreter, was killed. Consequently, the troops at El Fuerte del Cíbolo were put to work cutting poles to reinforce the stockade and raise its ramparts.[43]

Although no more specific information could be found in the extant Bexar Archives indicating that more cattle were

41. Cabello to Croix, September 14, 1780, Bexar Archives (BAT, 2C42, Vol. 102, 45-47).

42. Cabello to Croix, September 18, 1780, Bexar Archives (BAT, 2C42, 45-47).

43. Cabello to Croix, September 19, 1780, Bexar Archives (BAT, 2C42, vol. 102, 55-59).

trailed to Louisiana after the disastrous raid on Córdoba's herd, a muster roll fragment for the Presidio San Antonio de Béxar, dated October 20, 1780 (See Appendix), shows that one corporal and eleven privates were "in the cattle crew for the paymaster."[44] Presumably, they accompanied more cattle to Nacogdoches that fall in response to the urgent request of Gálvez for cattle for his troops in the campaign against Pensacola, which, because of another hurricane, was postponed till the spring of 1781.

Communications of November 20th and December 6th told of more troubles in Texas. An epidemic of disease afflicted the populace of both Béxar and La Bahía. Cabello stated that the Presidio de Béxar was without medication and anyone to administer it; nor was there anyone who could perform bloodletting to aid the uncountable number of sick people. Even Cabello himself had been fighting off fever that had left him unconscious for three days. He had just learned, too, that a large group of Lipan Apaches enroute to the Nueces River had been forced to stop ten leagues out of Béxar because of small pox and diphtheria, both striking at the same time. Not only were these wild Indians being decimated by disease, but even were the mission Indians dying in great numbers. While the epidemic raged in and around Béxar, Comanche Indians continued their hostilities by attacking Rancho del Paistle, which belonged to Mission Concepción.[45]

A last clue indicating a delivery of cattle in the winter of 1780-1781 is found in a fragment of a letter dated December 20, 1780. In it Cabello mentions meeting with Don Francisco Rosé, a French trader whom Gálvez had sent to promote free trade between the provinces of Texas and Louisiana. Suspicious of possible profiteering motives of Rosé, Cabello listed the reasons he opposed free trade:

44. Company of Cavalry at Presidio San Antonio de Béxar, October 20, 1780, Bexar Archives (BAT, 2C43, vol. 104, 53-55).
45. Cabello to Croix, November 20, 1780, and December 6, 1780, Bexar Archives (BAT, 2C44, vol. 106, 15-16 and 47-49).

. . . Considering that the object of such trade is to reap the benefits in La Luiciana of bovine and equine livestock, which are so scarce in that province, what will come to pass is that the year this project [free trade] is established these species of animals will be so scarce in this province [of Texas] that the case will arrive wherein a horse will be worth twenty *pesos* and a head of beef will bring twice as much. At that point it will be impossible to supply the presidios in the province of Coahuila—as matters are indeed turning out at the present. Cattle will become totally lacking, and none will be found even for our own sustenance. Surely no benefit will redound to this province, for in La Luiciana each head will be worth four fancy linen kerchiefs and some *maritatas*, and in order to acquire these items, people will take all their cattle to that land [Louisiana] to sell them at opportune times, at which each head will not fail to bring twenty *pesos*.

This province is already very scarce in cattle. The Lipan-Apaches have consumed great numbers; furthermore, the cattle have not multiplied as they might, because the people, terrorized by the hostilities of the hostile Indians, have been unable to devote themselves to attending their herds; and this neglect has brought about a great deterioration. I have found myself in the position of having to publish a *bando* providing for a fine of ten *pesos* for each cow taken to the province of Coahuila.[46]

According to Cabello, there had been quite a drain on the number of cattle in Texas, but he tempered his remarks so as not to limit the supply of cattle that Gálvez had requested. He continued:

46. Cabello to Croix, December 20, 1780, Bexar Archives (BAT, 2C44, vol. 106, 61-68).

In consequence of the obligation in which Your Lordship might find yourself with respect to the *cavallero* Don Bernardo de Gálvez, and in order that the supply of cattle he might need should not be limited—particularly in view of the royal order of May 1st, which Your Lordship enclosed for me in your official letter of the 6th of October—Your Lordship, if you should be pleased to, can grant the aforesaid *cavallero* governor whatever he might need for those ends that conduce to the welfare of that province [Louisiana]. Your Lordship affording me notice of what [number of cattle] is needed, I will apply every possible means to effect its most expeditious delivery.[47]

This was the last mention in the Bexar Archives about any kind of cattle delivery prior to Gálvez's Pensacola campaign, which lasted from March 9 to May 10, 1781. Although details are utterly lacking, there is indication that live cattle accompanied Colonel Joseph Ezpeleta's troops as they made the overland march from Mobile to join Gálvez at Pensacola. His nine hundred men had reached the Río Perdido on March 16th, and Gálvez ordered launches there to help them across. On April 5th, Gálvez had a meeting with the chiefs of the Talapuz Nation in which "the General listened to their mission, and it was agreed that they should supply the camp with fresh meat." The next morning Galvez dispatched the Talapuz chiefs on a mission to the English faction to persuade them not to take sides during the war "and to bring all the cattle they could."[48] One of the possibilities here would be that the Talapuz Indians would relieve Spanish soldiers of the chore of butchering beef for the troops.

A critical difference in the siege of Pensacola was that Gálvez's troops were well supplied with food, but the British had run short. George C. Osburn, in his description of the plight of General John Campbell at Pensacola, wrote:

47. *Ibid.*
48. Diary . . . Bernardo de Gálvez, 62-63.

. . . for some weeks no ships loaded with supplies had arrived at Pensacola. This fact, coupled with immense consumption of provisions by the Indians, with an added allowance of food for laborers who were working on defense projects, and the necessity of supplying some of the transports with victuals and with the maintenance of a large number of refugees, had caused a shortage of necessities.[49]

With the Pensacola campaign successfully completed, Gálvez set his sights on the conquest of Jamaica and the conquest of the Bahamas. His need for more provisions would continue for another year.

Bexar Archives records indicate no more cattle shipments until July 12, 1781, when Vizente Flores applied for permission to round up two hundred bovines for export to an undesignated destination, which could have been either Louisiana or Coahuila. One hundred unbranded bovines were rounded up at the places of La Sinfonía, Las Tetillas, Los Olmos, El Carrizo, and Los Nogales. The other hundred, rounded up at Rancho de las Mulas, had his own brand, that of his father, Don Francisco Flores, and that of his uncle, Don Tomás Travieso. The two hundred head were combined into one herd at the Rancho of Don Simón de Arocha, ready to be driven out. Guarantors for the payment of tax for the unbranded cattle were two citizens of Bexar, Don Francisco Flores and Juachín Flores. The export tax was set at twenty-five *reales* per head.[50]

One week later, two more applications were filed for permits to export cattle. On July 19th, Don Simón de Arocha, a citizen and militia commander of the *villa* and *presidio* at Béxar, petitioned to export three hundred head of cattle to Coahuila.[51]

49. George C. Osburn, "Major-General John Campbell in British West Florida," *The Florida Historical Quarterly* (April, 1949), XXVII, 337.

50. Vizente Flores to Cabello, July 12, 1781, Bexar Archives (BAT, 2C45, vol. 108, 89-90).

51. Simón de Arocha to Cabello, July 19, 1780, Bexar Archives (BAT, 2C45, vol. 108, 99-101).

On that same date, Juan José Flores applied for a permit to take 120 cattle to the Province of Coahuila.[52]

That fall, Don Joseph Antonio Curbelo, lieutenant governor of the Province of Texas, asked and received permission to export two herds totalling over one thousand head. On September 17, 1781, Curbelo was granted permission to round up a herd of six hundred unbranded cattle from the pastures around Los Nogales. Destination of the export was unspecified. Curbelo promised to secure the value of the cattle by the guarantees of two creditable persons and by pledging his own property.[53] A writ and decree dated October 9, 1781, affirmed that Sergeant Domingo Pérez had just come from the Rancho de las Cabras, where Curbelo had gathered another herd of 469 cattle for export. Again, no destination was given. The cattle were appraised at 22 *reales* per head.[54]

No further exports are mentioned in the Bexar Archives records until May 4, 1782, when Don Antonio Blanc, evidently a Frenchman, applied for a permit to gather 1200 cattle from the pastures of the arroyos of El Tulillo, Las Animas, and Los Nogales for export to the province of Louisiana. Antonio de la Garza, a resident of Béxar, was commissioned to count and certify the cattle, and Blanc was ordered to pay in hard cash the export fee of two *reales* for each animal he took.[55] Quite possibly, these cattle could have been intended to supply Gálvez's forces in the campaign against Jamaica, which was never carried out. And it was the last record of a cattle drive to Louisiana during the time period of this study.

52. Juan Joseph Flores to Cabello, July 19, 1781, Bexar Archives (BAT, 2C45, vol. 108, 64-65).

53. Joseph Antonio Curbelo to Cabello, September 17, 1781, Bexar Archives (BAT, 2C45, vol. 108, 137-138).

54. Writ and Decree, October 9, 1781, Bexar Archives (BAT, 2C45, vol. 108, 138 and 145-146).

55. Proceedings, May 4-July 30, 1782, Bexar Archives (BAT, 2C47, vol. 112, 10-13).

IV

SOME RAMIFICATIONS

Two centuries behind us, the American Revolution is still an exciting and relevant story. "The Shot Heard 'Round the World" reverberates even today. Ideas of human freedom were planted in men's minds. It has taken many years for them to find conditions conducive to germination and growth. The innate quest for human freedom continues.

Viewed from a Texas perspective, the American Revolution takes on a new dimension. A product of recent historical research, the Texas connection figures into the larger role that Spain played in the winning of American independence, which had world-wide repercussions. But only the surface of the roles of Spain, New Spain, and Texas has been scratched, and much more needs to be researched and written about this interesting aspect of the Revolution.

It is said that King George III and his ministers, in the silence following the last roll of war drums, pondered the reasons why they had lost the war. A roster of soldiers and ships couldn't explain it, for Britain had the biggest army and navy in the world. Rather, as one minister put it, Britain's real problem was that conquering America was like trying to conquer a map. The land that Britain claimed stretched across half a continent connected by rough roads from New England to West Florida and lay three thousand miles over an ocean whose fickle winds and currents might take messages and supplies across in a month.

And this is precisely where Spain figures in the story of Britain's defeat—and the colonists' victory. Most military strategists agree that much can be gained by opening a second or a third front against an enemy. George Washington and his

Continental Army provided the main thrust. A second front was maintained by George Rogers Clark and his men in the West. And the third front, which diluted the enemy's forces even more, was directed by Bernardo de Gálvez and his Spanish troops along the Gulf Coast. In addition to these three main fronts, Britain had to spread herself out all over the world and fight in such far-flung places as Nicaragua, the West Indies, Bermuda, the Azores, Cape Verde Islands, Senegal, off the British coast, Gibraltar, Minorca, Capetown, and even India. It was indeed a world war for England.

A critical factor in maintaining an effective military offense or defense is the line of supply. British supply lines were stretched out very thinly all over the world. Although the British erected a fairly effective blockade of the thirteen American colonies on the Atlantic side, they could not control the Gulf. Consequently, great amounts of military supplies were delivered to American forces by way of the backdoor—the Mississippi River—held open by Gálvez and his Spanish forces.

When Gálvez took to the field against the British in West Florida, his forces ranged from 1400 to 7000 men. When compared to the numbers of men who fought under American, French, or British commanders, this was a sizeable force. Cornwallis, for example, commanded an army of 6000 men when he surrendered at Yorktown. Contrary to modern notion, Spanish participation in the American Revolution was vital, direct, and considerable.

Food is a prime necessity of life that many people take for granted, especially in times of plenty. In time of war, however, it can be the critical difference between victory and defeat. A well-supplied, well-fed army will have the energy it needs for fighting. On the other hand, a poorly supplied and poorly fed army is half-whipped before it starts battle. Gálvez made sure that his men were abundantly supplied with food, and it paid off with victory after victory. Texas beef supplied some of the energy for Spanish soldiers, both during and between battles. In marked contrast, the British ran critically short on food, especially during the siege of Pensacola, which ensured their defeat.

Gálvez provided a line of supply to American forces. Whether fighting or not, men need to eat regularly, and cattle secured from Texas went a long way in providing food for Gálvez's men for the better part of three years.

Thus far, we know the story of Texas cattle in the American Revolution only from Bexar Archives sources. At best, the records are fragmentary and leave large gaps that could be filled by research in other Spanish documents in archives in Mexico, Cuba, and Spain. Hopefully, the time and occasion will arrive when a competent researcher will be able to corroborate these findings with the information that is sure to be found in other archival records. A significant addition would be made to the body of historical knowledge.

In summary form, Texas cattle in the following numbers were ordered and/or driven to Gálvez's forces:

1779
2000 — (ordered by Francisco García)
300 — (ordered by María de St. Denís)
970 — (delivered by Joseph Félix Menchaca)
???? — (ordered from Mission Rosario)

1780
???? — (delivered by Francisco Flores, Joseph Félix Menchaca, and Juan de Ysurieta)
1234 — (delivered by Marcos Hernández)
2000 — (ordered from Mission Espíritu Santo)
???? — (escorted by soldiers listed on October 20, 1780, Muster Roll)
???? — (ordered by Francisco Rosé)

1781
200 — (delivered by Vizente Flores)
1069 — (delivered by Joseph Antonio Curbelo)

1782
1200 — (delivered by Antonio Blanc)

8973 + — Total Number Ordered and/or Delivered

From the foregoing, it can be noted that nearly nine thousand head of Texas cattle were ordered or delivered for Gálvez. It appears that there were probably several thousand head more that cannot be ascertained at this time. And there is no telling how many cattle might have been ordered and delivered for which no record exists.

It should be remembered that many Louisiana cattle were killed by the hurricane in August, 1779, and part of the purpose of the imported Texas cattle was to restock Louisiana herds. Consequently, a number of bulls were sent along with the herds of cows and steers. Granted the biological facts that a cow can bear a calf each year and that a calf can reach sufficient size for slaughter in a year's time, natural propagation would add to the number of cattle that became available for Gálvez's army within the three-year war period.

Historians are still looking for all the places where "The Shot Heard 'Round the World" travelled. The innate quest for human freedom took a giant leap with the American Revolution, a leap that reached to France and then to Latin America. Some writers give convincing cases that we look not to America but to Bourbon France for the source of liberal ideas that permeated to Mexico and South America. That liberal thought from Voltaire, Montesquieu, Rousseau and others was transferred to New Spain through such men as Alzate, Abad y Queipo, and Hidalgo cannot be denied. But a source for the democratic ideal so long sought by Mexico and so often examined, thus far in vain, by historians is that of our own United States of America.

We now know what Spain did for the American Revolution. On the other side of the coin is what the American Revolution did for Spain. Spanish forces were very active in the affairs of the Revolution from 1776 to 1783, a time span of nearly eight years. During those years, over 7000 men, many of them coming from Louisiana, Texas, Cuba, the Canary Islands, and Mexico, participated in the American theatre. It is not inconceivable that many of them returned home espousing some of the ideals for which the war was fought. It is known, for example, that

Francisco Miranda served as one of Gálvez's officers in the campaigns at Pensacola, the Bahamas, and Jamaica. Miranda returned to Venezuela with the conviction that Spanish colonies to the south should follow the example of the thirteen American colonies. There were many Spanish officers and men besides Miranda, and ever so many could have returned to their homelands with new ideas of individual freedom. Their names are available to researchers in Spanish archival records. The American Revolution certainly gave the practical example—if not the idea—for the revolutions that rocked Mexico and South America the first part of the nineteenth century.

One Spaniard stands head and shoulders above all the rest—Bernardo de Gálvez. John Walton Caughey made a good start on a biography of this great man, but his complete life story is needed—and deserved. More research on the earlier and later life of Gálvez may show that he exuded considerable liberal influence upon his associates. It would be extremely interesting to know about his activities in detail, for example, while he was the viceroy of New Spain in 1785 and 1786. Liberal thought was fermenting in Mexico at this time, and he could have been one of the prime movers of the democratic ideal.

A Texas name that is steeped in revolutionary tradition is that of the Menchaca family. In a line of descent that is not clear, members of this family figured prominently in the American, Mexican, and Texas revolutions. Joseph Félix Menchaca, who delivered at least two herds of cattle to Louisiana, was directly involved in the American Revolution. It is quite possible that he met Gálvez in person while in New Orleans. Miguel Menchaca, probably the grandson of Luis Antonio and the great-nephew of Joseph Félix, served under Bernardo Gutiérrez de Lara during the Mexican Revolution in Texas. And a later descendant, José Antonio Menchaca, distinguished himself during the Texas Revolution in the siege of Béxar and at San Jacinto. The place of Manchaca in Travis County commemorates the name of this family.

Related to the Ramón and St. Denís families, who were also very prominent in the early history of Texas, the Menchaca family would provide a classical Texas example for researchers interested in a *peninsular vs. criollo* case study for Texas. Three Menchacas accompanied the Martín de Alarcón expedition that founded San Antonio de Béxar in 1718. Francisco Menchaca, one of Alarcón's soldiers, stayed and became one of the first settlers of San Antonio. His son, Luís Antonio Menchaca, was the captain of the Presidio San Antonio de Béxar from 1763 till his retirement about ten years later. Deep-seated animosities developed between the Menchacas and governors Barón de Ripperdá and Domingo Cabello. The Menchacas had lived in Texas for a long time, and they resented being pushed around by a self-righteous foreigner. The Menchacas were bred to the frontier, and they embodied ideas of rugged individualism and freedom that were both alien and irritating to both governors.

What is most important in this study is the historical justification it provides for both Spain and Texas in being deservant of recognition for their roles in the American Revolution. Americans of Hispanic descent can take great pride in the contribution of their forebears in the achieving of American independence, and they can directly identify with the great cause of human liberty.

A premise made at the beginning of this study was that we yet have much to learn in history. The story set forth here just barely scratches the surface of a greater story that needs to be told. Notwithstanding, it is the writer's hope that the start to a new dimension in American Revolution history has been added as a result of this study. It is also hoped that further research and writing on this subject will gain the recognition justly deserved by both Spain and Texas for their roles in the American Revolution. And, finally, it is earnestly hoped that someone—somewhere—sometime will fully describe the life and times of Bernardo de Gálvez, that great Spanish military and political figure of the American Revolution whose name is deserving of special honor by all Americans.

APPENDICES

APPENDIX A

Dec. 1, 1779

Cavalry Company of the Royal Presidio of La Bahía
del Esp[íri]tu Santo

Report and roster of the cavalry company which garrisons the above-cited royal presidio, listing names [of the men], whether they are present or absent, and the assignments of each one, in accordance with the provision of His Majesty in Title 9 of his Royal Regulations:
[P: present, CP: counted present]

Captain . . . D[on] Luis Cazorla . . . . CP.
                                     On inspection tour
Lieutenant . . . D[on] Josef Santoja . . . . P.
1st *Alférez* . . . D[on] Josef Aguilar . . . . P.
2nd *Alférez*
  of *tropa*
  ligera . . . D[on] Policarpo Prada . . . . P.
Chaplain . . . D[on] Josef Feliz Ramos . . . . P.
1st Sergeant . . Josef Fran[cis]co Básquez . . . . P.
2nd Sergeant
  of *tropa*
  lig[er]a . . . Francisco Borra . . . . P.
Drummer . . . Josef Andrés de Ribas . . . . P.
1st Corporal . . . Antonio Trebiño . . . . P.
2nd Corporal . . . Fran[cisc]o Ríos . . . . P.
Privates . . . Josef Contreras . . . . CP.
                                     On detached duty
Gerardo Flores . . . . CP.
                                   With the horseherd
Juan Guisar . . . . P.
Josef Flores . . . . CP.
                                   With the horseherd
Anacleto Ríos . . . . CP.
                                   With the horseherd

Ambrosio Higuera . . . . CP.
                                 With his captain
Ylario Maldonado . . . . .P.
Fran[cis]co Hernández . . . . CP.
                              With the horseherd
Eugenio de la Garza . . . . CP.
                                       Ill
Fran[cis]co Salas . . . . .P.
Antonio de la Garza . . . . .P.
Cayetano de los Santos . . . . CP.
                           Ill, in San Antonio
Antonio Albarado . . . . .P.
Juan Montalbo . . . . .P.
Juan Josef Martínez . . . . CP.
                              On detached duty
Alexo de León . . . . .P.
Casimiro Cano . . . . CP.
                               On guard duty
Esteban Salas . . . . .P.
Juan Bautista Cano . . . . CP.
                                       Ill
Andrés del Río . . . . CP.
                              With the horseherd
Fran[cis]co Ramón . . . . CP.
                              With the horseherd
Hermenegildo Gómez . . . . .P.
Josef González . . . . CP.
                                       Ill
Ygnacio Garzía . . . . .P.
Santiago Delgado . . . . .P.
Tomás de la Garza . . . . CP.
                              With the horseherd
Tomás Ortiz . . . . .P.
Bérnabe del Río . . . . CP.
                              With the horseherd
Juan Chirino . . . . CP.
                              With the horseherd
Miguel Bezerra . . . . CP.
                               With his captain
Mariano Tegeda . . . . .P.

Damasio Aldape . . . . CP.
Ill
Bernardo de la Garza . . . . CP.
Ill
Fernando Galán . . . . CP.
On guard duty
Josef Jabier Sains . . . . CP.
Ill
Antonio Bázquez I . . . . CP.
On guard duty
Jabier Maldonado . . . . CP.
With the horseherd
Josef Cayetano Zepeda . . . . CP.
Ill
Fran[cis]co Antonio Buentello . . . . CP.
On detached duty
Pedro de los Santos . . . . CP.
With the horseherd
Pedro Josef Grande . . . . CP.
On detached duty
Juan Augustín de la Garza . . . . P.
Antonio Bázquez II . . . . CP.
With the horseherd
Prudencio de San Miguel . . . . CP.
With the horseherd
Josef Timoteo Ximénez . . . . CP.
With the horseherd

Ymbálidos

Lieutenant D[on] Jabier Benites . . . . CP.
Absent with leave
Private Pedro Ceballos . . . . P.

Summary

Captain CP.1
On inspection tour
Lieutenant P.1

1st *Alférez* P.1
2nd *Alférez* of *tropa ligera* P.1
Chaplain P.1
Sergeant P.1
2nd Sergeant of *tropa ligera* P.1
Drummer P.1
First Corporal P.1
Second Corporal P.1
Privates with the horseherd CP.14
Ydem on guard duty CP.03
Ydem with their captain CP.02
Ydem as escort or on detached duty CP.04
Ydem in the garrison P.14
Ydem ill P.07
Ydem in San Antonio CP.01

Ill

      Total strength   55

Ymbálidos

Lieutenant d[o0n Jabier Benites CP.1

Absent with leave

Pedro Ceballos P.1

      General total   57

//²

[The above report] is certified by me [Fernández] as commander of this royal presidio, and by the lieutenant and the *alférezes* of the company under their command which garrisons [the presidio].

Eugenio Fernández	José Santoja	José Aguilar
[Rubric]	[Rubric]	[Rubric]

Policarpo Prada
[Rubric]

//2V [Blank]   [D.S., 1-2 pp., 12/1/1779]

	Sergeants	Drummer	Corporals	Privates	Armorer	Total
[With the] horseherd	1		2	30		33
[At Cíbolo] Fort			1	19		20
With the paymaster			1	03		04
[In the] cattle crew for the paymaster			1	11		12
With the mail			1	06		07
Ill	2			05		07
On guard			1	07		08
Available for duty, at the governor's orders	1	1	1	01	1	04
Totals	3	1	8	82	1	95

Service details in which on today's date is engaged the 95-man troop that constitutes the cavalry company at the said presidio.

Note
From the four men // 1V available for duty, the drummer and the armorer should be excluded; whence it will be seen that there remain only 2 men available for duty; consequently the 8 men on guard have to stand long watches, and hence all the men at the other posts have to remain at them without relief.

Royal presidio of Béxar, October 20, 1780.

[Remainder—apparently a first draft—inverted:]

	Sergeants	Drummer	Corporals	Privates	Total
[With the] horseherd	1		2	30	33
[At Cíbolo] Fort			1	19	20
With the paymaster			1	03	04
With the mail			1	06	07
Ill	2			05	07
On guard			1	07	08
Available for duty		1	1	02	09
Men who were in the cattle crew for the pay- master			1	11	12
Totals					95

[D., 1-1v pp., 10/20/1780]

BAT 2C45, Vol. 109 — January 2, 1782

Synopsis of the review passed on the officers, sergeants, drummer, corporals, and privates of this company for the month of January, 1782, by Colonel in the Royal Armies Don Domingo Cabello, governor and commander of arms of the province of Los Texas and captain of the afore-mentioned company, in conformity to that which is prescribed by His Majesty in article 3, title 9 of the regulations and instructions issued for the administration of presidios on the frontier line of the Interior Provinces of this kingdom of New Spain.

Captain . . . . Colonel Don Domingo Cabello, governor and commander of arms of the said province, as captain of this company   Present

1st lieutenant . . . Don José Menchaca . . . . Detached in the province of Coahuila

2nd same . . . Don Bernardo Fernández . . . . Present

1st *alferes* . . . Don Marcelo Váldéz . . . . Sick

2nd same . . . Don Fran[cis]co Amangual . . . . Present

Chaplain . . . . Vacant

Persons [illegible]

1st sergeant . . . Manuel de Urrutia . . . . On detached duty at the fort of El Cíbolo

2nd same . . . Domingo Peres . . . . Present

1st corporal . . . Pedro Peres . . . . Present

Another of the same . . . Andrés de Valle . . . . Detached, in Coahuila for the *estanco*

2nd corporal . . . José Ant[oni]o Flores . . . . Detached, at the fort of El Cíbolo

Another of the same . . . Fran[cis]co Xavier de Sosa . . . . Detached, with the horse herd

Privates . . .

Cadet . . . Don Nicolás Lemé . . . . Present

Domingo Diego Acosta . . . . Detached, with the horse herd

Juan Remigio de Torres . . . . Detached, with the same

Martín de Castro . . . . Detached, with the same

Antonio Gonzales . . . . Detached, at the fort of El Cíbolo

Fran[cis]co de Sales Games . . . . Sick

Alexando Ydalgo . . . . Detached, with the mail

Juan María de la Cerda . . . . Detached, at the fort of El Cíbolo

Facundo Mansolo . . . . Present

Antonio Baca . . . . Detached, in Coahuila for the *estanco*

Xavier Zepeda . . . . Detached, with the mail
Juan Casanoba . . . . Detached, in Coahuila
for the *estanco*
Fernando de Arocha . . . . Detached, with the
horse herd
Carlos Hernandes . . . . Sick
Francisco Sánchez . . . . Detached, at the
fort of El Cíbolo
Juan Chirino . . . . Sick, at the presidio
of [San Juan Bautista
del] Río Grande

//1V

Fran[cis]co Ant[oni]o Urrutia . . . . Detached, at the
fort of El Cíbolo
Pedro Manzolo . . . . Detached, in Coahuila
for the *estanco*
Juan Ant[oni]o de Urrutia . . . . Detached, with the
horse herd
Francisco de Castro . . . . Detached, with the same
José Farías . . . . Detached, with the same
Manuel Ramón . . . . Detached, with the same
Francisco Losoya . . . . Detached, with the same
Fran[cis]co Sales de la Cerda . . . . Detached, at the
fort of El Cíbolo
Patricio Rodríguez . . . . Detached, with the
horse herd
Juan Ant[oni]o Casanoba . . . Detached, with the same
Juan José Bueno . . . . Present
José Manuel Granados . . . . . . Detached, with the mail
Antonio Martínez . . . . Detached, with the
horse herd
Cristóbal Guerra . . . . Detached, with the mail
Manuel Salinas . . . . Detached, with the
horse herd
Manuel de Castro . . . . Detached, with the same
Man[ue]l Leandro Martínez . . . . Detached, at the
fort of El Cíbolo
Jazinto Ramón . . . . Detached, with the mail
Armorer . . . Francisco Orendain . . . . Present

Persons in the *tropa ligera*

3rd sergeant . . . Mariano Rodríguez . . . . Detached, with the horse herd

Drummer . . . Juan José Calderón . . . . Present

1st corporal . . . Francisco Camacho . . . . Present

Another of the same . . . Prudencio Rodríguez . . . . Present

2nd corporal . . . Juan José Sánchez . . . . Detached, with the mail

Another of the same . . . Francisco de los Santos . . . Detached, with the horse herd

Privates . . . Lorenzo Flores . . . . Sick

Pedro Flores . . . . Detached, with the horse herd

Manuel Flores. . . . . Present

Pablo de la Garza . . . . Detached, with the horse herd

José Agustín Hernandes . . . . Detached, with the same

José Gil de Leyoa . . . . Detached, with the same

Pedro Hernández . . . . Detached, with the same

Bizente Gonzales . . . . Detached, at the fort of El Cíbolo

Mathías de la Garza . . . . Detached, at the same

Bonifacio Hernandes . . . . . Detached, with the horse herd

Eusebio de la Garza . . . . Detached, at the fort of El Cíbolo

Lázaro de Torres . . . . Detached, with the horse herd

Mariano de la Garza . . . . Sick

José María Uraga . . . . . Detached, with the horse herd

José Joaquín Peres . . . . Present

Juan José Córdoba . . . . Detached, with the horse herd

Francisco Ant[oni]o Leal . . . . Detached, with the same

José Bruno Menchaca. . . . . Detached, at the fort of El Cíbolo

José Ant[oni]o Baquera. . . . . Sick

José Miguel Sánchez . . . . Sick

José Ant[oni]o Gomes . . . . Detached at the fort of El Cíbolo

José María Olibarri . . . . Detached, with the horse herd

José Fran[cis]co Padilla . . . . Present

José Manzolo . . . . Detached, with the horse herd

87

Juan Cadena . . . . Sick
Pedro Ant[oni]o Ortiz . . . . Sick
Ygnacio Flores . . . . Detached, at the fort of El Cíbolo
Ygnacio Peres . . . . Present
Tomás de Luna . . . . Detached, with the horse herd
José Flores . . . . Present
José Ant[oni]o de la Garza . . . . Detached, at the
fort of El Cíbolo
Pablo del Río . . . . Detached, at the same
Pedro José Enrique . . . . Detached, at the same
Juan José Cadena . . . . Detached, at the same
José de la Garza . . . . Detached, with the
horse herd
Manuel Berbán . . . . Present
Bentura Rico . . . . Detached, with the horse herd
Diego Carmona . . . . Present
Pedro Montalbo . . . . Detached, with the horse herd
José Alexandro de la Garza . . . . . Detached, with the same
Pedro Chirino . . . . Detached, with the mail
José de Sosa de Rosas . . . . Present
Fran[cis]co Xavier Peres . . . . Detached, at the
fort of El Cíbolo
Marcelo Borrego . . . . Detached, at the same
José Fran[cis]co de Villafranca . . . . Present
José de Arocha . . . . Present
José Ramon Flor[e]s de Ábrego . . . . Detached, at the
fort of El Cíbolo
Andrés Courbiere . . . . Present

Ymbálidos

Alferes . . . Don Juan José Ydalgo . . . . Present
Sergeant . . . Pedro Granados . . . . Present
Privates . . . Pedro Miñón . . . . Present
Bartholomé Rosales . . . . Present
Manuel Villarreal . . . . Present
José Miguel Games . . . . Present

//2V

88

Summary

Captain . . . . Present: 1
1st . . . Lieutenant . . . . Detached, counted present: 1
2nd . . . Same . . . . Present: 1
1st . . . *Alferes* . . . . Sick counted present: 1
2nd . . . Same . . . . Present: 1
Chaplain . . . . Vacant:
Total 5

Persons *de cuera*

1st . . . Sergeant . . . . Detached, counted present: 1
2nd . . . Same . . . . Present: 1
1st . . . Corporal . . . . Present: 1
Another . . . Same . . . . Detached, counted present: 1
2nd . . . Corporal . . . . Detached, counted present: 1
Another . . . Same . . . . Detached, counted present: 1
Privates present 4
Detached . . . . counted present: 28
Sick . . . . counted present: 3
Total 47

Tropa ligera

3rd . . . Sergeant . . . . Detached, counted present: 1
Drummer . . . . Present: 1
1st . . . Corporal . . . . Present: 1
Another . . . Same . . . . Present: 1
2nd . . . Corporal . . . . Detached, counted present: 1
Another . . . Same . . . . Detached, counted present: 1
Privates present 11
Detached . . . . counted present: 31
Sick . . . . counted present: 6
Total 54
Active total 100
Ymbálidos 6

General total 106

Note

That Lieutenant Don José Menchaca is in the province //³ of Coahuila by provisions of the governor of this [province], who has advised the lord commandant general; hence in the review [Menchaca] is listed as being on detached duty.

Royal Presidio of San Ant[oni]o de Béxar, January 2, 1782.

Dom[ing]o Cabello
[Rubric]

//3V [Blank]   [D.S., 1-3 pp., 1/2/1782]

BAT 2C47, Vol. 112 — May 1, 1781

Cavalry Company of the Royal Presidio of La Bahía del Espíritu Santo

---

Report of the review passed on the officers, chaplain, sergeants, drummer, corporals, and privates of this company for the month of May, 1782, by Lieutenant Don José Santoxa, interim commander of this presidio, in accordance with that which is prescribed by His Majesty in article 3 of title 9 of the royal regulations and instructions issued for the establishment of the presidios on the frontier line of the Interior Provinces of this kingdom of New Spain.

Captain . . . Don Luis Cazorla ....Counted present, on commissioned assignment in Coahuila

Lieutenant . . . Don José Santoxa ....Present

1st ensign . . . Don Policarpo Prada............On detached duty at San Luis [Potosí] for the allowance

2nd *Yd[e]m* . . . Don Antonio de Méscières...............Present

Chaplain . . . B[achille]r Don José Félix Ramos ....Present

Troops *de cuera*

1st Sergeant . . . Francisco Vásquez.......................Present

1st Corporal . . . Francisco Ríos ....Present

Another *Yd[e]m* . . . Bernavé del Río....................Present

ño . . . . Present

ario Maldonado . . . . . On detached duty
with the horse herd

On detached duty with the horse herd

. . . . Present

detached duty with the horse herd

. . . . On detached duty at San Luis
for the allowance

Alvarado . . . . Present
Alexo de León . . . . Present
Andrés del Río . . . . On detached duty with the horse herd
Hermenegildo Gomes . . . . On detached duty with the horse herd
Thomás Ortís . . . . Present
Miguel Vezerra . . . . Present
Mariano Texeda . . . . On detached duty with the horse herd
Fernando Galán . . . . On detached duty with the horse herd
Antonio Vásquez . . . . Present
Xavier Maldonado . . . . Present
Pedro de los Santos . . . . . . On detached duty with the horse herd
Pedro José Grande . . . . Present
Agustín de la Garza . . . . Present
Prudencio de San Miguel . . . . Present
José Dionicio Liendro . . . . Present
José Antonio Conejo . . . . . On detached duty with the horse herd
Juan José Games . . . . Present
Juan José de León . . . . Present
Vincente Zerna . . . . Present
Armorer . . . José Cayetano de Zepeda . . . . Present

Ligera Troops

2nd Sergeant . . . Antonio Treviño . . . . On detached duty with
the horse herd
Drummer . . . José Andrés Ribas . . . . Present
1st Corporal . . . Francisco Buentello . . . . On detached duty at San
Luis with the paymaster
Another *Yd[e]m* . . . Francisco Ramón . . . . Present
2nd Corporal . . . Bernardo de la Garza . . . . Sick

91

Another *Yd[e]m* . . . Anacleto Ríos . . . . On detach
the

Privates . . .
José María Ramón . . . .
Francisco de la Garza . . . . . On detached duty with the horse
Diego Chirino . . . . On detached duty at San
with the paymaste
Justo López . . . . On detached duty with the horse herd
Diego de los Santos Cadenas . . . . Present
Francisco Xavier Vásquez . . On detached duty with the horse herd
Marciano Treviño . . . . Present
Francisco Venites . . . . On detached duty with the horse herd
Jacinto Martines . . . . Present
José Manuel de la Garza . . . . Present
Pedro Treviño . . . . Present
José Gil . . . . Present
José Polinario Péres . . . . Present
Juan Nepomuceno Aldape . . . . Present
Manuel Narciso Venites . . . On detached duty with the horse herd
Antonio Margil Venites . . . . Present
Antonio Ramón . . . . Present
Sevastián Maldonado . . . . Present
Joachín Galán . . . . On detached duty with the horse herd
Antonio del Río . . . . Present
Juan Andrés Contreras . . . . Present
Thomás Macías . . . . Present
José Leonardo Ramón . . . . Present
Juan Flores . . . . Present
Pedro José Texeda . . . . Present
Carlos Delgado . . . . On detached duty with the horse herd
Pedro Antonio de Luna . . . On detached duty with the horse herd

Ymválidos

Lieutenant . . . Don Xavier Venites . . . . Present
Private . . . Pedro Zevallos . . . . Present
/ /²

Summary

```
    Captain ................... Detached, counted present: 1
    Lieutenant ............................... Present: 1
1st ... Ensign ................... Detached, counted present: 1
2nd ... Yd[e]m ............................... Present: 1
    Chaplain ............................... Present: 1
  Total ................................................ 05
```

Troops *de cuera*

```
1st ... Sergeant ................................ Present: 1
1st ... Corporal ................................ Present: 1
Another ... Yd[e]m ............................. Present: 1
2nd ... Corporal ............................... Present: 1
Another ... Yd[e]m ............... Detached, counted present: 1
    Privates at this presidio with the armorer .......... Present: 15
    Privates .................... Detached, counted present: 9
  Total ................................................ 29
```

Ligera Troops

```
2nd ... Sergeant ................ Detached, counted present: 1
    Drummer ................................... Present: 1
1st ... Corporal ................. Detached, counted present: 1
Another ... Yd[e]m ............................. Present: 1
2nd ... Corporal .................................. Sick: 1
Another ... Yd[e]m ............... Detached, counted present: 1
Privates at this presidio ........................... Present: 9
Privates ....................... Detached, counted present: 18
  Total ................................................ 33
Active total .......................................... 67
Ymválidos ............................................ 02
General Total ........................................ 69
```

This I certify as interim commander of this company, [as does] Don Antonio de Mézcières, 2nd ensign of the same; at this Royal Presidio of La Banía del Espíritu Santo, today, the 1st of May, 1782.

José Santoja   Antonio de Mésières
[Rubric]   [Rubric]

/ / 2V
[Blank]   [D.S., 1-2 pp., 5 / 1 / 1782]

CAVALRY COMPANY of the Royal Presídio of La Bahía del Espíritu
Santo, May 5, 1782. These original documents provided by the Perry-
Castañeda Library. The University of Texas at Austin.

Compañía de Cavalleria del R.l Prev.io de la Bahia del Espiritu Santo

Extracto de la Reuista pasada à los Oficiales Capellan Sargentos tambor Caves
i Soldados de esta Compañia perteneciente al Mes de Mayo de 1782 por el Sen.te
D.n Jose Santoxa Comandante Ynterino de este Prev.o arreglado á lo prevenido
por S.M. en el Art.o 3.o del tit.o 9.o del Real Reglamento é instrucion expedida p.a el Establec.to
de los Premicios en la Linea de Frontera de las Proas internas de Este Reyno de N.E.

Capitan	Don Luis Cazorla	CP Comunicado en Coahuila
Teniente	Don Jose Santoxa	
1.er Alferz	Don Policarpo Prada	D en San Luis por el Cruzado
2.o Alm	Don Ant.o de Mescieres	P
Capellan	Br D.n Jose Felix Ramos	P

Tropa de Cuera

1.o Sargento	Francisco Vasquez	P
1.er Cave	Francisco Rios	Ps
Otro Ydm	Bernave del Rio	P
2.o Cave	Juan Chirino	R
Otro Ydm	Jose Ylario Maldonado	D en la Cauallada
Soldados	Jose Contreras	D en la Cauallada
	Jose Flores	
	Eugenio ata Ganza	D en la Cavallada
	Francisco Salas	D en San Luis por el Cruzado
	Antonio Alvarado	R
	Alexo de Leon	P
	Andres del Rio	D en la Cauallada
	Hermenegildo Gomez	D en la Cauallada
	Thomas Ortis	P
	Miguel Vezerra	P
	Mariano Texeda	D en la Cauallada
	Bernando Salan	D en la Cauallada
	Antonio Vasquez	P
	Xavier Maldonado	P
	Pedro de los Santos	D en la Cauallada
	Pedro Jose Grande	B
	Agustin de la Garza	P
	Prudencio de San Miguel	P
	Jose Dionicio Liendro	P
	Jose Antonio Conejo	D en la Cauallada
	Juan Jose Gomes	P
	Juan Jose de Leon	P

94

	Vicente Ycarra	P
Armero	Jose Caietano de Cepeda	P

Depá Yserra

2.º Sargente	Antonio Treviñi	D en la Cauallaca
tambor	Jose Andres Ribas	P
1.º Cauo	Francisco Buenreello	D en San Luis en el Hacilu.º
e n.º Ylm	Francisco Ramon	P
2.º Cauo	Bernardo de la Suana	E
e n.º Ylm	Anicldo Rios	D en la Cauallaca
s oldados	Jose Maria Ramon	P
	Francisco de la Sarra	D en la Cauallaca
	Diego Chirino	D en San Luis en el hacilu.º
	Juro Lopez	D en la Cuuallada
	Diego de los Santos Cadenas	P
	Francisco Xavier Vasquez	D en la Cuuallada
	Marciano Treviño	P
	Francisco Venies	D en la Cauallada
	Jacinto Martino	P
	Jose Manuel de la Sarra	P
	Pedro Treviño	P
	Jose Gil	P
	Jose Solmanio Peres	P
	Juan Nepomuceno Aldape	P
	Manuel Narciso Venies	D en la Cauallada
	Antonio Marcil Venies	P
	Antonio Ramon	P
	Sevastian Maldonado	P
	Joachin Sutan	D en la Cauallada
	Antonio el Rio	P
	Juan Andres Coroneros	P
	Thomas Macias	P
	Jose Leonardo Ramon	P
	Juan Siores	P
	Pedro Jose Tereda	P
	Carlos Welgado	D en la Cauallaca
	Pedro Antonio de Lunan	D en la Cauallada

Ymvalidos

| | Luis Xavier Venies | P |
| | | P |

Resumen

Capitan . . . . D C P , }			
Teniente . . . . P , }			0 5
1º . . . . Alferes . . . D C P , }			
2º . . . . Idm . . . „ P „ }			
Capellan . . . . P }			

tropa de Cuera

1º . . . . Sargento . . . P , }			
1º . . . . Cabo . . . „ P „ }			
Uno . . . . en . . . „ P „ }			
2º . . . . Cabo . . . „ P „ }			29
Uno . . . . Idm . . . D C P „ }			
Echados en este tiem con el Arm . . . „ P 3 5			
Soldados . . . . . D C P „ 9			

tropa Ligera.

2 . . . . Sargento . . . D C P „ }			
Tambor . . . . „ „ P „ }			
1º . . . . Cabo . . . D C P „ }			
Uno . . . . Idm . . . „ P „ }			33
2º . . . . Cabo . . . „ „ E }			
Uno . . . . Idm . . . D C P „ }			
Soldados en este Presº . . . „ „ P „ 9			
Soldados . . . . . D C P „ 8			
Total Efectivo . . . . . „ „ „ „ „ „			67
Ynvalidos . . . . . „ „ „ „ „ „			0 2
total General . . . . . „ „ „ „ „ „			69

Lo que Certifico como Comandante Ynterino de esta Compañia
Dn Antonio de Mezieres 2º Alferes de la misma en este Rl
Presº de la Bahia del Espiritu Santo oy 1 de Mayo de 1782.

Jose Sandoval   Antonio de Mesieres

INDEX

Acadian Coast: 28
Alarcón, Martín de: 53, 78
Algiers: 23
Álvarez, Juan: 28
Amite River: 29
Antioch, Texas: 5
Armas, Lorenzo de: 15
Arocha, Chepe: 16
Arocha, Estanislao: 16
Arocha, Juan de: 15-16
Arocha, Julian de: 16
Arocha, Simón de: ranch of, 15-16, 71; as militia commander, 71
Arroyo del Cíbolo: 12-14
Arroyo de los Nogales: 63, 71; roundup at, 65-66, 72
Atascosa County, Texas: 12
Ávila, Blas de: 16
Ávila (Spain), Military School of: 23
Azores: 74

Bahamas: campaign against, 40, 42; capture of, 47
Barrera, Juan: 15
Baton Rouge: English post at, 27; campaign against, 29; battle at 46
Bayou Manchac: 30
Belmont, Texas: 13
Bermuda: 74
Betancourt, María Robaina de: 15
Béxar: SEE San Antonio de Béxar, Presidio de Bexar Archives: ranch records of, 10; muster rolls in, 56; mentioned: 50, 67, 70-72, 75
Blanc, Antonio: 72, 75
Bodore, Monsieur: 51
Boiderout, Mr. de: 38
Bonet, Juan Bautista: 61
Borbón y Borbón, King Juan Carlos Victor María de: 3

Bormé, Louis Jean Césaire: 52
Bucareli (village): SEE Nuestra Señora del Pilar de Bucareli
Bucareli y Ursúa, Antonio María (Viceroy): 4
Bueno, Juan: 16
Buentello, Francisco Antonio: 56

Cabello, Domingo: as governor, 4; residence of, 51; authorizes first cattle drive, 46; correspondence of, 48-49, 54-59, 61, 63, 64, 68; troubles with ranchers, 59-61; grants permit, 63; laments losses, 66; returns to Béxar, 67; opposes free trade, 68-70; difficulties with the Menchacas, 78
Cagigal, Juan Manuel: as field marshal, 38; captures Bahamas, 40, 42
Cahokia: 27
Calvillo, Ignacio: ranch of, 14, 16
Calvo de Irazabal, Joseph: as commander of fleet, 35-36; mentioned, 38
Camargo, Nuevo Santander: 9
Campbell, John: as commander, 33-34; correspondence with, 37; surrenders, 39; plight of, 70-71
Canary Islanders: settle San Fernando, 6; ranches of, 13; settle at Bayou Manchac, 30
Canary Islands: recruits from, 28, 76
Capetown, South Africa: 74
Cape Verde Islands: 74
Carlos III (King): as king, 3, 19, 24; issues "New Regulations," 4; secret loan by, 26; rewards Gálvez, 40; commissions

Gálvez, 45; royal order of, 58
Carrizosa, Felipe López: 38
Casanova, Joseph Pérez: 16
Casanova, Manuel: 16
Casa Reales: as governor's residence, 6, 51
Castelo, Domingo: 16
Castro, Marcos de: 16
Catherine the Great: 3
cattle kingdom: 10; SEE ALSO cattle
cattle: role of in American Revolution, 18, 45, 47; trail drives of, 45-46, 50, 62-63; regulations on, 47-48; bulls delivered, 49, 51, 76; needed in Louisiana, 58; ordered by Gálvez, 59, 63, 76; delivered to Opelousas, 60; at Mobile, 61; bought from Espíritu Santo, 63; as food supply, 74-75
Cazorla, Luís: as captain, 56; retirement of, 67
Chester, Peter: 37
Chihuahua: in Nueva Vizcaya, 1, 20, 46. SEE ALSO Nueva Vizacaya.
Cibolo Creek: SEE Arroyo del Cíbolo
Clark, George Rogers: aid to, 26; campaigns of, 27-28; second front by, 74
Coahuila: cattle exports to, 48, 71-72; military party in, 53; SEE ALSO Nueva Estremadura
Collegio de San Gregorio: 22
Colorado River: 60
Contreras, Josef: 56
Concepción, Mission: SEE Nuestra Señora de la Purísima Concepción
Córdoba, Cristóbal Ylario de: cattle drive by, 64-65
Cornwallis, Lord Charles: 47, 74

Courbiere, Andrés Benites: ranch of, 16
Croix, Marqués de (Viceroy): 20, 22
Croix, Teodoro de (Caballero): as *comandante-general,* 5; correspondence of, 48-49, 52-54, 57-59, 62-64, 66; decree of, 47-48; *bando* by, 54; establishes mail service, 56
Cuba: recruits from, 76
Cuellar, Lope de: 20
Curbelo, Joseph Antonio: as rancher, 16; named interim governor, 57; as lieutenant governor, 72; cattle delivered by, 75
Czestochowa, Texas: 5, 14

Delgado, Clemente: 16
Delgado, Jazinto: 16
Delgado, Doña Leonora: ranch of, 15
Delgado, Manuel: ranch of, 14-16
De Mézières, M.: 52
Dickson, Alexander (Lt. Col.): at Fort Bute, 29; at Baton Rouge, 30; at Fort George, 37
Dolores, Nuevo Santander: 9
Durán, Torivio: 16
Durnford, Elias (Capt.): at Fort Charlotte, 33

East Florida: 26, 42
El Capote: 13
El Carrizo: 71
El Cíbolo: SEE Santa Cruz del Cíbolo, El Fuerte de
El Monte del Diablo: 63
El Paso: SEE Paso del Norte, Presidio del
El Rincón: 13-14
El Tulillo: 72
England: SEE Great Britain
Escandón, José de: 8

Escobar, Fray José María de: 64
Espíritu Santo, Mission: SEE
    Nuestra Señora del Espíritu
    Santo de Zuñiga, Mission
Ezpeleta, Joseph (Colonel): at
    Mobile, 34; overland march of,
    35; placed in command, 37;
    captures "The Crescent," 39;
    march to Pensacola, 36-37;
    cattle with troops of, 70

Falls City, Texas 14
Ferdinand VI (King): 3
Fernández, Bernardo de: 67
Flores, Cano: 16
Flores, Francisco: activities of,
    60-61; as citizen of Béxar, 71;
    cattle delivered by, 75
Flores, Gerónimo: water spring of,
    65
Flores, José Francisco: 16
Flores, Joseph Juachín: 16
Flores, Juachín: 71
Flores, Juan Joseph: ranch of,
    15-16; applies for permit, 72
Flores, Phelipe: 63
Flores, Vizente: as rancher, 16;
    cattle delivery by, 71, 75
Flores de Ábrego, Francisco: ranch
    of, 15-16
Floresville, Texas: 14
Fort Barrancas Coloradas: 28, 35,
    36, 39
Fort Bute: campaign against, 28-29;
    58
Fort Charlotte: campaign against,
    32-33; 59
Fort George: campaign against,
    37-40
Fort Panmure: surrender of, 30
Fort Pitt: 24, 26
Foucher, José: 63-64
France: Gálvez in, 22; declares war,
    45

Franco, Francisco: 3
Frederick the Great: 3
Fuerte del Cíbolo: SEE Santa Cruz
    del Cíbolo, El Fuerte de

Gallardo, Josefa: as mother of Ber-
    nardo de Gálvez, 19
Gálvez, Antonio: as uncle of Ber-
    nardo de Gálvez, 19-20
Gálvez, Bernardo de: family of, 4;
    life of, 19; military career of,
    20-23; as governor of Loui-
    siana, 23-24; promotions of,
    20, 22-23, 31, 33, 40; aid to
    Americans, 25-27; welcomes
    Willing, 27; military plans of,
    28; attack on Fort Bute, 29;
    attack on Baton Rouge, 30;
    completes campaign in Loui-
    siana, 31; campaign against
    Mobile, 32-33; campaign
    against Pensacola, 33-40;
    wounded, 22, 37; campaign
    against Bahamas, 40, 42; later
    career of, 42-43; death of, 43;
    commissioned by king, 45;
    campaign against Apaches, 22,
    46; Gulf Coast campaign of,
    46-47; letter from, 48; letter
    about, 61; as governor, 49; let-
    ter to, 52; receives news of
    declared war, 54; campaign of
    1779-1780, 58; cattle ordered
    by, 59, 63-64, 68, 70; opens
    third front, 74; forces of,
    74-75; as unsung hero of the
    American Revolution, 77-78
Gálvez, José de: as uncle of Bernar-
    do de Gálvez, 19-20; letters
    by, 23, 54-56
Gálvez, Matías de: as viceroy, 4; as
    father of Bernardo de Gálvez,
    19; in Nicaragua, 38; death of,
    42

Gálvez, Miguel de: as uncle of Bernardo de Gálvez, 19
Gálveztown (ship): 36
Gálveztown (village): 30
García, Francisco: as emissary, 46, 48-50; mentioned, 52; returns to New Orleans, 57; cattle ordered by, 75
Garza, Antonio de la: 72
Garza, Joseph Martín de la: ranch of, 16
Garza, Juachín de la: ranch of, 16-17
Garza, Leonardo de: 17
Garza, Martín de la: 17
Garza, Miguel de la: 17
Gayarré, Juan Antonio: 32
George III (King): 3, 73
Georgia: prisoners return to, 39
German Coast: 28
Gibraltar: 74
Gibson, George: mission of, 24-26
Gila River: campaign at, 22
Girón, Gerónimo: as brigadier general, 38; captures "The Crescent," 39
Goliad, Texas: 7, 10; SEE ALSO Nuestra Señora de Loreto de la Bahía, Presidio de
Gonzales County, Texas: 13
Gortari, Miguel de: ranch of, 16-17
Granado, Pedro: 17
Grande, Pedro Josef: 56
Grand Pré, Carlos: 29
Great Britain: Spain declares war against, 27, 45, 54; world war for, 73-74
Guadalupe River: ranches along, 12-13; Comanche depredations along, 64
Guerra, Francisco: 17
Guerra, Mariano: 17
Guerra, Miguel: ranch of, 15, 17
Guerrero, Félix: 60
Gustav III (King): 3

Havana, Cuba: bureaucrats in, 32; fleets from, 32, 35; reinforcements from, 34; brig from, 37-38; expedition from, 40
Halifax, Nova Scotia: contemplated attack on, 42
Henry, Patrick: letters by, 26
Hernández, Andrés: land grant of, 13-14
Hernández, Francisco: 17
Hernández, Joseph Andrés: 17
Hernández, Joseph Placido: 17
Hernández, Marcos: cattle delivered by, 63, 75
Holland: declares war, 45
horses: delivered to Louisiana, 46, 52; bought in Nuevo Santander, 66
Hortega, Juachín: 52

India: 74
Indians: Apaches, 20, 22, 46; Lipan Apaches, 68; Comanches, 51, 63-68; Talapuz, 70

Jamaica: mentioned, 39; proposed campaign against, 42, 47
Jefferson, Thomas: 26
Junta de los Ríos Norte y Conchos, Presidio de la: settlement at, 9; ranches near, 10

Karnes County, Texas: 5
Kaskaskia: 27
Kosciusko, Texas 13-14

La Bahía: SEE Nuestra Señora de Loreto de la Bahía, Presidio de
Lake Pontchartrain: actions on, 30
Gutiérrez de Lara, José Bernardo: 77
Laredo, Nuevo Santander: 1, 9
La Sinfonía: 71

Las Animas: 72
Las Tetillas: 71
Leal, Juachín: 17
Lee, Charles (General): letter from, 24-25
León, Alonso de: 53
Los Adaes: as capital of Texas, 2
Los Nogales: SEE Arroyo de los Nogales
Los Olmos: 71
Longoria, Francisco (Colonel): 38
Louis XVI (King): 3
Louisiana, Province of: governor of, 19; instructions for governing, 23; cattle trailed to, 46, 72; need for Texas cattle, 58; recruits from 76
Louisiana Regiment: 23

Macharaviaya, Spain: 19
Malaga, Province of (Spain): 19
Manchac: as English post, 27; attack on, 29, 46; march to, 58; SEE ALSO Fort Bute
Manchaca, Texas: 77
Maria Theresa (Empress): 3
Martínez, Carlos: ranch of, 15, 17
Martínez, Juan Josef: 56
Martínez, Luciano: 17
Mathe, Nicolás de la: as trader, 50
Maxwell, John: as governor of Bahamas, 40
Mayorga, Martín de (Viceroy): 4, 61
Medina County, Texas: 12
México: recruits from, 28, 76
Minorca: 74
Menchaca, Francisco: as first settler: 53, 78
Menchaca, José Antonio: in Texas Revolution, 77
Menchaca, Josef Félix: as lieutenant at Béxar, 6, 17, 52-53, 57; cattle delivered by, 51, 53-54, 75; activities of, 60-61; pursues

Comanches, 65; transferred, 67; involvement in American Revolution
Menchaca, Juachín: 17
Menchaca, Luís Antonio: land grant of, 13-14; as rancher, 17; as presidial captain, 53, 78
Menchaca, Miguel: mentioned, 52; in Mexican Revolution, 77
Miranda, Francisco: as aide-de-camp to Bernardo de Gálvez, 40, 77
Miró, Estevan: 62
Mississippi River: gunpowder sent up, 25; war material sent up, 26; activity on, 27; flood of, 58; as backdoor to American Revolution, 74
Mobile: instructions concerning, 31; British attempt to regain, 34; campaign against, 32-34, 46, 58, 61-62; reinforcements from, 37; SEE ALSO Fort Charlotte
Mobile Bay: 32
Mobile Point: 32
Monclova, Nueva Estremadura: 1
Monjarás, Sebastián: 17
Móntes, Joseph María: 17
Móntes, Marcos: 17
Morris, Robert: as financier of revolution, 27
Mathe, Nicolás de la: as trader, 50
Miró, Estevan: 62

Nacogdoches: ranches near, 10; mentioned, 18, 50; cattle trailed to, 46, 51, 64, 68; herd at, 52; sent news of declared war, 55-56; SEE ALSO Nuestra Señora del Pilar de los Nacogdoches, Villa de
Natchez: as English post, 27; operations against, 29, 46; surrender at, 30; SEE ALSO Fort Panmure

Natchitoches: cattle trailed to, 46, 54; mentioned, 50; herd at, 52

Navarro, Diego, Joseph: as captain-general of Cuba, 61

New Mexico: SEE Nuevo México, Province of

New Orleans, Louisiana: as a part of New Spain 1; Americans seek aid at, 24-26; military supplies from, 27; prisoners at, 31; fleet from, 32, 35; forces return to, 34; reinforcements from, 37; mentioned, 50, 52, 57; visited by *Tejanos*, 60; courier from, 61

New Providence, Bahamas: capture of, 47

New Regulations: 9

New Spain: SEE Nueva España

Nicaragua: 67, 74

Nueces River: as boundary, 1, 8; ranches along, 10

Nuestra Señora de la Purísima Concepcíon, Mission: census for, 7; lands of, 12; ranch of, 15, 68

Nuestra Señora del Espíritu Santo de Zuñiga, Mission: census for, 7-8; lands of, 13; cattle from, 50, 63-64, 75

Nuestra Señora de Loreto de la Bahía, Presidio de: establishment of, 5; census for, 7-8; ranches near, 10; mentioned, 18, 50; cattle near, 46; soldiers from, 46; monthly rosters of, 56; sent news of declared war, 55-56; Cabello at, 57-58, 66; epidemic at, 68

Nuestra Señora del Pilar de Bucareli: settlement of, 5, 8; ranches near, 10

Nuestra Señora del Pilar de los Nacogdoches, Villa de: settlement of, 5; census for, 8; SEE ALSO Nacogdoches

Nuestra Señora del Rosario, Mission: census for, 7-8; lands of, 13; ranches of, 15; cattle from, 50, 57, 75

Nueva España: territorial limits of, 1; viceroyalty of, 4

Nueva Estremadura, Province of: boundaries of, 1, 9; SEE ALSO Coahuila

Nueva Vizcaya, Province of: boundaries of, 1; settlement of, 9; military actions in, 20, 22; SEE ALSO Chihuahua

Nuevo México, Province of: boundaries of, 1; description of, 10

Nuevo Santander, Province of: boundaries of, 1, 9; colony of, 8-9; cattle driven to, 48; horses from, 66

Oconór, Hugo: as *comandante-inspector*, 5; replaces Gálvez, 22

Ohio River: activity on, 27

Ojinaga, Chihuahua: 9

Opelousas, Louisiana: cattle trailed to, 46, 50-51, 60, 63; mentioned, 52

O'Reilly, Alejandro: 23

Orosco, Julian de: 60

Osburn, George C.: 70

Pacheco, Juan Joseph: bulls belonging to, 51; mentioned, 52

Padrón, Manuel: 17

Panis, Jacinto: spy mission of, 31-32

Panna Maria, Texas: 14

Paso de la Laja: 13

Paso del Norte, Presidio del: establishment of, 9; ranches near, 10; new deputy governor for, 67

Pecos River: fight at, 20, 22, 46

Peña, Joseph Ygnacio de la: ranch of, 15
Peña, Ygnacio: 57
Pennsylvania: 26
Pensacola: instructions concerning, 31; British reinforcements from, 33; campaign against, 33-40, 61, 70-71; siege of, 35-40; capture of 47; mentioned, 61; SEE ALSO Fort George
Pensacola Bay: 35
Pérez, Domingo: 72
Pérez, Francisco: cattle driven by, 51
Pérez, Juan Ignacio: ranch of, 16
Pérez, Juan Manuel: ranch of, 16
Pérez, Luís: ranch of, 16
Perú: viceroyalty of, 4
Philadelphia, Pennsylvania: 25
Philip V (King): 3
Pickles, William: 30
Piernas, Pedro: as commander of Louisiana forces, 35
Pineda, Manuel (Colonel): 38
Piscina, Manuel Ramírez de la (Captain): ranch of, 15
Pollock, Oliver: influence of, 25; as supporter of American Revolution, 27; as aide-de-camp, 28; letter from, 30; in Cuba, 42

Queen's Redoubt: 38-39; SEE ALSO "The Crescent"

Rada, Joseph: 34
Ramírez de Arellano, Fray Pedro: as *presidente* of Texas missions, 49; letter from 64
Ramón, Diego (Captain): 53
ranches: in Texas, 9-18; as an institution, 10;
—Rancho de Gertrúdis Rodríguez: 16
—Rancho de Lagunas de las Animas: 14

—Rancho de la Mora: 14, 51
—Rancho de las Cabras: 14, 72
—Rancho de las Hermanas: 16
—Rancho de las Mulas: 15, 65-66, 71
—Rancho de los Chayopínes: 15
—Rancho del Atascoso: 16
—Rancho del Capitán: 15
—Rancho del Diesmero: 15
—Rancho del Paistle: 15, 68
—Rancho del Paso de las Mujeres: 14
—Rancho de Nuestra Señora de la Candelaria de las Calaveras: 15
—Rancho de Palo Quemado: 15
—Rancho de Pataguilla: 14
—Rancho de San Antonio del Cíbolo: 15
—Rancho de San Cristóbal de Espanta Perros: 15
—Rancho de San Bartolomé: 14, 65-66
—Rancho de San Francisco: 14, 51, 53, 60-61
—Rancho de San José de los Alamos: 15
—Rancho de San Lorenzo de las Mulas: 15
—Rancho de San Lucas: 16
—Rancho de San Miguel de Amoladeras: 15
—Rancho de San Rafael: 15
—Rancho de San Yldefonso de Chayopín: 15
—Rancho de Santa Cruz de la Laja: 15
—Rancho de Señor San José: 15
Rattletrap (ship): 26-27
Red River: 1
Regiment of Cantabria: 22
Regiment of Havana: 32
Regiment of Louisiana: 32
Regiment of Principe: 32

Regiment of Seville: 22-23
Reñe, Lorenzo: 60
Rentería, Cayetano: 17
Revilla, Nuevo Santander: 9
Reynosa, Nuevo Santander: 9
Riano, Juan: 37
Río Grande: settlements along, 8-9; ranches along, 10
Riojas, Carlos: 17
Río Pánuco: 1
Río Perdido: 36
Ripperdá, Juan María Vicencio, Barón de: as governor, 4, 54; and El Fuerte del Cíbolo, 57, 67; difficulties with Menchacas, 78
roads: as land boundaries, 13
—Béxar to Nacogdoches road, 51
—La Bahía road, 13
—Laredo road, 13
Robeline, Louisiana: 2
Rodríguez, Diego Yrineo: ranch of, 15
Rodríguez, Francisco: 17
Rodríguez, Francisco Xavier: ranch of, 16-17
Rondein, Julian: 67
Rosario, Mission: SEE Nuestra Señora del Rosario, Mission
Rosé, Francisco: as trader, 50, 52; sent by Gálvez, 68; cattle ordered by, 75
Ruíz, Agustín: 60
Ruíz, Juan Manuel: ranch of, 16

Sabine River: ranches along, 10
Salinas, Pedro Xavier: 17
San Antonio, Texas: SEE San Antonio de Béxar, Presidio de, AND San Fernando de Béxar, Villa de
San Antonio de Béxar, Presidio de: capital at, 3; establishment of, 5-7, 10, 78; description of, 6;

census for, 7; ranches near, 10; mentioned, 13, 18, 50, 52; cattle near, 46; letter arrives at, 48; officer at, 51; soldiers from, 46; cattle from, 54; receives news of declared war, 55-56; monthly rosters of, 56, 68; contraband at, 61; epidemic at, 68
San Antonio de Valero, Mission: census for, 7; ranches of, 14; lands of, 12: cattle from, 51
San Antonio River: presidio near, 7; missions along, 7; ranches along, 12-14
San Carlos, Nuevo Santander: as capital, 1
Sánches, José: 17
San Eleazario, Presidio de: 9
San Fernando Cathedral: 6
San Fernando de Béxar, Villa de: civil settlement of, 5; description of, 6-7; census for, 7; receives news of declared war, 56
San Francisco de la Espada, Mission: census for, 7; lands of, 13; ranch of, 14
San José y San Miguel de Aguayo, Mission: census for, 7; lands of, 12-13; ranch of, 16
San Juan Bautista del Rio Grande, Presidio de: settlement at, 9; new officer for, 67
San Juan Capistrano, Mission: census for, 7; lands of, 12; ranch of, 14
San Lorenzo: mission at, 10
San Pedro Creek: mission near, 12
Santa Cruz del Cíbolo, El Fuerte de: establishment of, 5; men stationed at, 6; mentioned, 18; soldiers from, 46; road by, 51; soldiers at, 52; visited by

Cabello, 57, 67; Comanche raids at, 65-66; no reinforcements for, 66
Santa Fé, Nuevo México: as capital, 1
Santa Rosa Island: 35-37
Santo Domingo: 40
Santoja, José (Lieutenant): 67
Saucedo, Joseph Antonio: 17
Seguín, Santiago: 17
Senecú: mission at, 10
Senegal: 74
Sigüenza Point: 35-36
Socorro: mission at, 10
Solano, Joseph: as commander of fleet, 38
Sosa, Joseph de: 17
Soto, Manuel de: 17
Spain: North American land claims of, 1; Gálvez returns to, 22; interest in American Revolution, 22, 24-26; declares war on England, 27, 45; 54-56; role in American Revolution, 42, 73-74, 78; effects of American Revolution on, 76-78
Spanish Governor's Palace: as comandancia, 6, 51, 53
St. Augustine, Florida: 40, 42
St. Denís, Doña María de: cattle ordered by, 54, 75

Tamaulipas: SEE Nuevo Santander, Province of
Texas, Province of: boundaries of, 1-2; description of, 5, 18; census for, 7-8; ranches of, 10-18; cattle of, 46; lieutenant governor of, 72; recruits from, 76
"The Crescent": 38-39
Thompson's Creek: 29
Travieso, Chico: 17

Travieso, Juan Andrés: 17
Travieso, Francisco: ranch of, 15, 17
Travieso, Tomás: ranch of, 15-16; as rancher, 17, 71; pursues Comanches, 65-66
Travieso, Vizente Álvarez: ranch of, 15, 17
Treaty of Paris of 1783: 42
Trinity River: ranches along, 10; crossing on, 51

United States of America: asks Spain for aid, 25; cites Bernardo de Gálvez for his aid during American Revolution, 42
Unzaga, Luís de: as governor, 23-25
Urrutia, José de: 53
Urrutia, Toribio de: 53

Váldez, Marcelo: 65
Venezuela: 77
Veracruz, México: 22, 42, 61
Villebeuvre, Juan de la (Captain): 30
Vincennes: 27
Virginia: 25-26

Washington, George: aid sent to, 26; served by Pollock, 27; defeats Cornwallis, 47; and Continental Army, 73-74
Webb, Walter Prescott: 10
West Florida: as arena of American Revolution, 26-27, 74; British capital in, 33; governor of, 37; ceded back Spain, 42
West Florida (ship): capture of, 30
West Indies: 74
Willing, James: expedition of, 26-27
Wilson County, Texas: 13

Ximénez, Albert: cattle trailed by, 51

105

Ybarbo, Antonio Gil: as settlement leader, 8; cattle inspected by, 51; letters to, 52, 64; as lieutenant governor, 56
Yorktown, Battle of: 47, 74
Ysleta, Nuevo México: mission at, 10
Ysurieta, Juan de: cattle delivered by, 50-51, 75; at Natchitoches, 52; activities of, 60-61

Zambrano, Macario: ranch of, 15
Zambrano, Joseph Macario: 17
Zepeda, Marcos: 17
Zerda, Joseph Francisco de la: 17